The High School Baseball Hitter's Handbook

The High School Baseball Hitter's Handbook

A guide through the high school years for baseball players and parents

Dylan Nasiatka

Copyright © 2021 Dylan Nasiatka
All rights reserved.
ISBN-13: 9798701223644

Table of Contents

Introduction *1*

    Section I: Getting Up to Speed 3

Chapter One: Welcome to High School *5*

Chapter Two: Why are You Playing? *9*

Chapter Three: Become a Great Teammate *15*

Chapter Four: What is My Coach Looking For? *19*

    Section II: Training for Your Opportunity 27

Chapter Five: Get into a Routine *29*

Chapter Six: Strength Training *37*

Chapter Seven: Hitting, Throwing, Defense *43*

Chapter Eight: Games are Overrated *53*

    Section III: Shining When the Spotlight is On 61

Chapter Nine: You're the Best *63*

Chapter Ten: Planning for Success on Gameday *67*

Chapter Eleven: Show it Off *79*

Chapter Twelve: Reflect on Your Performance *85*

    Section IV: Preparing for Whatever is Next 95

Chapter Thirteen: Do You Want to Play College Baseball? *97*

Chapter Fourteen: Managing the Recruiting Process *109*

Chapter Fifteen: The Path of Improvement *115*

Chapter Sixteen: Final Thoughts *121*

Acknowledgements *127*

References *129*

Introduction

I'm not here to tell you I have found a step-by-step program to share with you that will guarantee you success. I'm also not going to tell you I'm the best coach and the utmost authority in coaching that is here to deliver the gold standard for baseball books. What I have decided to do with this book is to take conversations and concerns I am hearing from parents and players at or around the high school level and to offer solutions to those concerns. This book is for the high school player who is driven to improve before entering or while actively enrolled in high school or for parents with children who are in this age group.

For the players reading this book, I want you to know that it is the highly driven players like yourself that make my career as a coach so enjoyable. The motivation for this book began several years ago, while I was playing baseball in college. I always knew I would want to write a book that gave back some of the information that helped me, but I wasn't reminded of this goal until my experiences throughout the year 2020.

The pandemic of 2020 reminded me that the most important things in life are family, friends, and passion for the things you choose to do. While staying inside and avoiding people, I realized how fortunate I am to have an occupation that I truly love. I know that you have passion for the game of baseball if you are taking the time to read this. Take this passion and keep running with it. You're going to be different than others you play baseball with if you take the extra effort to become a great player, but it will be worth it. Also, use this passion to connect to your teammates and your family. You'll never know when you'll need support from them, or the other way around.

For parents reading this, I believe the contents of the book can serve as a positive conversation starter. You're spending more time with your son or daughter than any coach, so your questions and affirmations can help your child much more than a coach in most cases.

This book will be divided into four sections: Getting Up to Speed, Training for Your Opportunity, Shining When the Spotlight is On, and Preparing for Whatever is Next. If you are already in high school and have experience playing baseball, you may find it useful to skip the first section and start immediately on the second section. I stand behind each word in this book as a lesson I have been taught in my own life, but if you are having difficulties with any of the topics in the book for whatever reason, please follow the contact information at 661hit.com and let me know.

Section I: Getting Up to Speed

Chapter One: Welcome to High School

The time has finally come, you have made it to high school. This is a time of excitement and anxious energy and one where you have a new opportunity to make an impact. Although you may feel like your anxiousness is limited to yourself, the rest of your peers are feeling similar feelings. As you are entering high school with some interest in playing baseball, you will want to start to take some steps to make sure you have an opportunity to make the team. Locations and districts will vary in their rules and regulations, but within the first week of school you should start taking steps to give yourself the best possible high school baseball career.

Agenda #1: Who is the Varsity Coach?

The first thing on your list of tasks is to find out who leads the baseball program at your school. Although you may not play varsity baseball as a freshman, you need to learn the name of the varsity coach and meet them within the first week. If they are not a teacher on campus, reach out to them in the most appropriate way via phone call or email. If you are planning on playing sports in the fall or winter, it is still best to reach out to the coach and meet them. Ask the coach when the tryout process begins, if there are any offseason workouts, and what types of programs you can get involved in to improve your game. You'll want to learn the coach's expectations as well, so you are fully prepared. Your school may have workouts starting in the fall or may have nothing until the spring, but you will want to know by talking to the varsity coach in the first week of school.

Agenda #2: Meet Other Players.

The second thing on your agenda is to meet some other players within the first week. You may know some of the players from prior relationships, but if you are new to the area or have changed school districts you may not. Talk with and listen to your classmates as some of them may reveal that they are baseball players. Look for other athletes when you are walking around campus. When you find other players, tell them you are interested in baseball and you might be able to coordinate some workouts together. Making some early connections with fellow baseball players can really pay off as you can start to work on your game earlier than some of your other classmates who may not be as aggressive in finding a new partner to play catch with.

Agenda #3: Go to the Meetings.

High school coaches will often schedule meetings during the first week of school for prospective athletes. If you want to play other sports, go to the meetings for those sports. The odds of playing two sports in the exact same season typically aren't all that great, although if you are good and the games don't conflict many coaches will look to find a way to make things work. Go to the meetings and make sure you are on time to them. After the meeting, shake the coach's hand and introduce yourself. Don't expect your coach to know your name after this meeting, but you want your face to be in the group as much as possible so don't miss out on the meetings.

Agenda #4: Tell Your Counselor.

It is a good idea to talk with your high school counselor early in the high school process about your plans to play baseball in high school. Sometimes your counselor can help with information about the sport, but they may also set you up in a P.E. class that better suits an athlete rather than one dedicated to the general student population. Your counselor is a valuable asset in high school, and they will help you with your class schedule and work to ensure you are on track to achieve your academic goals.

Agenda #5: Be a Good Student.

Shame on me for not writing this first, but it is extremely important that you start high school on the right foot. Your academics are the most important part of your time in school because without good enough grades, you'll be ineligible to play baseball. Stay engaged in the classes you are in and give a good effort. Most colleges have a rule that the athletes must sit in the first two rows in each of their classes and this is a good habit to adopt for yourself in high school. Although there will be many temptations from other students to slack in class, you must stay on top of your schoolwork to ensure you'll have a chance at getting on the field. If you are ever struggling in a class, talk to your teacher or counselor and they will help you.

Agenda #6: Meet Friends.

High school is an opportunity to meet new people. You won't like all of the people you meet, but as you start to talk to people in your classes you may develop some bonds. There are going to be people who will do things that won't be in your best interest like skipping class, drugs, or alcohol, but there are many who won't get into these things as well. Don't feel pressured to get into any peer groups for status or coolness. Try to be friendly to everyone but spend more time with those you share common goals with. Finding good friends takes some time so don't feel like you need to have all your friends established immediately.

After your first week of high school, you will start to settle into the groove of things. You will be busy if you are playing a fall sport and also trying to get involved with baseball activities. You may be playing on a team outside of high school and this may be the time you will need to pick between the two for practices if they both schedule at the same times. I generally recommend choosing the high school practice unless your coach makes a disclaimer to attend other events rather than the high school practice. If you are seeing a private coach on the side, make sure the scheduling doesn't interfere with any high school activities.

The following sections of the book will talk about some of the specifics of the game as a hitter and ways you can develop yourself into a better player. Your four years of high school represent nearly 1,400 days and choosing to get started on a path to improvement as early as possible gives plenty of time to become the player you are dreaming to become. Whether you are reading this book as a player, parent, or coach this book can act as a guide to developing habits to become great. It is uncommon for young high school players to take initiative to become great and by reading this you have already put yourself in a very select group.

Chapter Two: Why are You Playing?

One question people often forget to ask before starting a new endeavor is 'Why?' There are many different things to do while you are in high school from clubs to playing in the band. Although you will have time throughout high school for new activities and hobbies, playing baseball will be a time commitment that you may or may not be ready to begin. Rather than spending time playing a sport you don't enjoy, ask yourself, "Why am I playing?" You may not have a crystal-clear answer to this question, but the important thing is that you have a valid reason for beginning this journey.

Starting from a place of strong motivation can be a positive, but I don't believe it is completely necessary. There are some who continue to play baseball because they have some skill and are good at the sport, while there are others who love every part of the game and don't have much success. Whether you are talented or not, if you are choosing to play baseball you are giving yourself a great opportunity. With this said, to continue to excel at baseball, you may need to look inside for some extra motivation for when the game deals you a difficult hand. Some of the reasons people play include:
- Winning a varsity championship
- Getting a college scholarship
- Becoming popular at school
- Only there because parents made you
- Enjoying the time with teammates

- Just wanted to try it out
- Wanting to play baseball professionally someday
- Because you're good at it
- You like watching baseball on TV
- Enjoying playing the game of baseball

None of the reasons listed above are completely wrong or right for playing the game of baseball in high school. The key, however, lies within your ability to give a solid effort to your game. The nature of the game of baseball is a team game that is built with individual moments. Other team sports like basketball, football, or soccer rely on multiple individuals for success during possessions or plays. In other team sports, when one individual fails, there is likely another opportunity or another teammate that can clean up a mistake and avoid total disaster – like a missed pass to one teammate that gets caught by another teammate. Baseball rarely offers a safety net for the plays in the game and if the shortstop misses a grounder between his legs the runner usually ends up on base from the error. Your chances during the game are an individual opportunity to shine and your success then helps to drive team success.

Once you have figured out why you are playing, you can get started with things. Use the list of agendas from chapter one to build some relationships and do what you can to start improving your skills. One common theme you will read in this book is that your efforts to get better will start to give you more enjoyment for baseball, regardless of your reasons for starting to play. After you have your reasons for playing, come up with some goals. Goal setting can be scary, but a solid goal can be a great tool to help keep things clear. A few things about those who reach lofty goals:

They have a Growth Mindset

A growth mindset, simply put, is the idea that you can improve yourself continually throughout your entire life. This includes your athleticism and baseball ability as well as your intelligence. Those with a growth mindset view life as a process of growth and improvement without fear of failure, getting worse, or embarrassment. Using a growth mindset will serve you much better than a fixed mindset, which is viewing yourself as having fixed traits or characteristics that will forever remain the same. A growth mindset may be the most important trait for those who want to get the most out of life and the body they were given.

Wanting it Isn't Enough

Sitting around and daydreaming about the lights at Fenway or your at-bat in game 7 is great, but nothing gets accomplished without action. The key to improvement is consistent and purposeful practice. Get out there and do something every day that improves your game.

Set Action Goals

Getting to the MLB is a performance goal. So are hitting .300 and making your all-star team. Action goals are the steps you are going to take to get to those performance goals. For instance: "In order to hit .300, I am going to work on my fitness for 45 minutes per day, hit 35 balls off the curveball machine per day, and visualize success for 10 minutes per day in addition to the things I am already doing."

Take Baby Steps

Don't expect to be an overnight success and go from never hitting homers to leading the league. If you focus on the process and your action goals you will start to see improvements along the way, but it may be several weeks, months, or years before the improvements are noticeable compared to where you started. Try to improve small things consistently and they will compound into tremendous growth.

Stop Comparing Yourself

It doesn't matter what the other players on your team or area are doing, especially at the younger amateur levels. Compare yourself to yourself only and look to improve what you are doing through taking those action steps.

Assess Frequently

As you begin purposefully practicing to improve your game, it is important that you are checking your progress. After each at-bat you can take a moment to recall your swing decisions to help you with your game strategy, after each practice you can check to see if you need more or less of a workload, after each week you can analyze your performance to figure out if you need to slightly tweak your training, and so forth. Working with your head down and staying in the moment is a great idea during the session, but in the times where you aren't actively working on your game it is a good idea to keep track of your progress.

Surround Yourself with Winners

This should go without saying, but some people are winners, while others are simply losers. Winners work hard and will help others as they work for their own goals. Losers have selfish interests and won't look out for your interests. If your friends don't share similar goals to yours or if they are inhibiting your growth, find new friends.

Be Different

Success at the highest level is extremely uncommon. This means that if you are doing the same things as others you play with, you are likely not going to get to the highest level. If you go out of your way to improve and you talk about your dreams of reaching the pinnacle of the sport of baseball you will probably hear negative talk from many people who will say you won't make it. Don't worry; once you're at the top you'll be around a lot of people who went through the same struggles and dealt with being different, just as you did.

Go All-In

The fastest and most efficient way to improve is to give it your all. This doesn't only mean running as hard as you can on ground balls or giving your best effort in the weight room. Going all-in means that you are working as if your only option is to get to the MLB with no back-up plan. Those that go all-in obsess about getting to the MLB and make life choices that help them along that path. Side note: no back-up plan doesn't give you an excuse to do poorly in school. Learning as much as you can and earning good grades will help you in your journey to the big leagues.

And one more thing, it isn't about you at the end of the game. The win or the loss is pinned to the team, but during your training, practice, and in game it is all about you to help your team win more games. Do the best you can personally and be selfish with your personal time and development so you can give your team a great chance to win.

Chapter Three: Become a Great Teammate

Team sports offer very unique experiences for athletes and coaches. Shared joy and misery, while striving for a common goal, can bring out the best and worst in team members. It is those members of the team who best navigate emotional times who can stand out and leave a positive impact on the others around them. I want to pull on the thread of becoming a good teammate and give some ideas for how to achieve this. Let's look at one of the greatest teammates in the modern era of baseball, Derek Jeter, to see what we can learn.

When Derek Jeter was born, it is highly unlikely that the doctor congratulated his parents by saying, "*Congratulations, you've got a beautiful great teammate baby!*" What's more likely is that Jeter learned the values of becoming a good teammate just as other notoriously great teammates did before him. He learned these values as a young person and player and continued to model those values throughout his career. Jeter was known as the consummate leader. The guy you would want in your foxhole if it was hitting the fan. It isn't difficult to find glowing reviews of Jeter from his previous teammates. The respect given to Derek Jeter was earned through countless hours and years.

So, let's first look at the values we can pull out of the statements about Jeter. David Cone said, "You are the most even-keeled, turn-the-page-type player I have ever been around." Tino Martinez said, "He never made any excuses if he was hurt or injured." Andy Pettitte said, "A couple of things separated you from all the other players I played with — and I played with a lot of great, great players. One was the will to win and the intensity you took to the field every day. Another was how you were always so steady."[1] Even-keeled, check. No excuses, check. Will to win and intensity, check. Take those and add steadiness and you have a highly respected player. A great teammate.

The values Jeter showed are fantastic and the reason they are notable is because they AREN'T COMMON. Sports inspire emotion and the ability to maintain your cool in the face of failure, while still being connected to the moment, is hard. Want to practice that? Go play ping pong with your buddies and try your best to win. When you make a mistake, don't change your body language at all. Just keep playing. Yeah, that one is hard, but it is a start.

To become a great teammate, you need to first become responsible for yourself. Accepting responsibility for yourself is the first step in becoming a leader of others. In fact, whether you know it or not, you're already a leader even if that means you're only leading yourself. To become better at leading yourself, you need to become responsible for yourself. That means no more excuses. Make a pact with yourself now and stop making excuses. For anything. Follow Lamar Jackson's statement when you play bad, catch an unlucky break, or simply aren't getting the results you want. Nobody cares, work harder.

The values of the best teammates will remain constant because they are so difficult to attain and demonstrate. However, I want to switch gears a bit to talk about the main thing good teammates do. They add value.

The most common way to add value in athletics, and the way most celebrated in professional athletics, is to play well. While speaking of great teammates, it is often overlooked that they are contributors to winning because of their play. And if the great performances are in practice, that works too. One of the best teammates to ever play collegiate basketball was named

Swen Nater. He was recruited to play basketball at UCLA with the knowledge he would be the backup to Bill Walton and was arguably one of the best centers recruited that season. It was the drive to be great all the time that made Nater a legend on his team and in college basketball and was a contributor to winning two national titles while at UCLA. Nater practiced against Walton harder than any opponent Walton faced during the year and challenged him every day. It was Nater's hard work in practice and performance in his limited minutes on the court that may have pushed Bill Walton and UCLA over the edge to win those national championships. Great teammate.

Talking positively and improving the mood of the team are great things to do when you are watching from the dugout. Accepting the idea that you aren't going to play so your athletic performance never matters is a trap. Your performance always matters. Swen Nater never started a game at UCLA. Oh, and he went on to have an 11-year professional career. The important thing is that you contribute to the team with your performance, somehow. Work at your craft so when your chances come you have the opportunity to be a good teammate.

To tie this back together, let's look back at the values of Derek Jeter. Intense, steady, and no excuses. You can't fake passion and intensity to win. The best teammates have intensity because they care about winning. They do the things in practice to push their teammates like Swen Nater. Becoming a good teammate doesn't mean SABOTAGING yourself for the team. It means being your best possible you for your team. And doing everything you can so that you don't let your teammates down. Your high school coach is looking for those players who can be good teammates. Becoming a responsible person who is committed to helping the team and others is a difficult task, but one that is a skill in life that can lead you to success in more than baseball. The world can always use another great teammate.

Chapter Four: What is My Coach Looking For?

Quite possibly the most confusing part of moving to a new team, for players, is to determine the new coach's wants and needs for the team. I can remember, very vividly, all the coaches I played for and all the different styles they brought to the table. I also remember the ways I felt and reacted to criticism and feedback from each of these coaches. As a player, I was very focused on playing well, but more focused on winning. I was observant and responsive to each coach that I had and wasn't the type of player who immediately said 'yes' to everything the coach asked. I didn't say 'no' to things for no reason, but my concern was winning and if there was an instance where the coaching wasn't, in my opinion, going to lead to winning I often asked for better clarification from the coach. I was a 'difficult' player, because I wanted to know why the things we were doing were going to help our cause as a whole.

In my career as a coach, I am still questioning 'why' for the methods. Now, however, I also work with players who have the same types of questions I had as a player. Honestly, most coaches would rather the player who blindly follows directions than the player who asks extra questions frequently. Whether it is from insecurity that the player is challenging the coach or from simply wanting control over players, not every coach appreciates players who are constantly weighing the methods of each coach and thinking critically about the messages. So, using my experience as a 'difficult' player and as a coach who has had many different players with different personalities, I'm hoping this will help you to deal with coaches in a more positive way than some of my own experiences.

I did get along well with some of my coaches. These coaches were highly prepared, respectful to the difficulty of getting better, and gave me a feeling of trust that I would make decisions that helped myself and my team. The coaches with whom I didn't get along well seemed to work off emotion, degraded players on a personal level, and consistently gave me the feeling that my efforts were inadequate. The longer you play, the higher the probability that you will have coaches on both ends of the spectrum and everywhere in between. The bottom line is if you want to play, you must learn to work with and not against your coaches, regardless how they go about their business.

Coaches are going to make observations about you as a player and person from your first interaction with them. They'll look at your body size and try to assess your fitness level before ever seeing you move on the baseball field, in most cases. When you do get onto the field, your coach will start looking at players to determine who will be a best fit for the varsity, junior varsity, and freshman levels if your school fields all of those. When on the field, it is a good idea to wear proper baseball gear at practice including baseball cleats, baseball socks, baseball pants, a baseball belt with your school color, an appropriate shirt (P.E. shirt works), and a hat worn forward. Some coaches may allow slightly relaxed uniforms in practice, but to ensure a good impression show up in full proper attire for try-outs and practices until told otherwise. If you don't have any of the items needed, talk to your friends or coach about borrowing some. Although the first assessment will likely look at your body, the subsequent assessments will likely analyze your agility, strength, speed, and baseball-specific abilities. Some high school try-outs resemble a showcase to display each player's tools (hitting ability, hitting power, speed, defensive ability, arm strength). It is extremely hard, in a small sample of a couple days, to make perfect decisions especially if the group of players is large. Many times, players will be moved to different teams based on grade level before anything else.

When trying out, stick to the position you feel is your best. If you have always wanted to switch positions, the first day of tryouts might not be the best time. Most times you will have some practice days before the games begin, so if you are good enough to help the lineup your coach may move you to a different position to give you more playing time. Be optimistic about moving positions and give all these suggestions your best effort. You will have time during the summer and fall months to work on your own at a different position if you are wanting to make a change, but the priority for you in the high school season should be to help the team win and keep improving as much as possible.

An important skill with your coaches and in life is to make eye contact when talking with others. If your coach is speaking to the group, look them directly in the eye. If you speak directly with the coach, look them directly in the eye. This skill takes time to develop, but when you look at your coach, it ensures you are listening to them. Give your coaches your full attention when they speak, because the information they are giving is to help your game.

Some coaches will have an idea to build a lineup a certain way if they have the players to do it. The coach may prefer a defense-heavy approach, a speed-oriented approach, or a power approach to deciding who he wants to play among many other types of lineup structures. Many schools don't have the option to create a highly specialized lineup, but it is a great idea to learn about your coach to figure out what his or her preferences are for a lineup.

The next step after your coach looks at the players and ability levels, is they will likely begin to coach you and give feedback. The best way to improve yourself and to become a player your coach wants to play is to correct the mistakes he or she observes. The feedback you receive and your ability to take that feedback and improve your skills can become a major separator between players who get on the field and those who are watching from the dugout.

What is feedback?

Feedback is the message you receive because of some action, or inaction. Feedback includes criticism, although within the team environment there are 'constructive criticism,' which is given to you from somebody within your organization or circle of trust, and 'destructive criticism,' which is from somebody outside your organization and circle. Constructive criticism may be blunt or even rude, but if it is from your coach or people you trust it is generally for a positive purpose. Destructive criticism doesn't have a purpose of helping you and is just noise that should be blocked from your mind such as heckling.

Your coach wants to win!

Although there are some issues with travel baseball where players may be given preferential treatment based on non-playing merits, high school baseball coaches generally put the best players and lineup on the field to win games. Once you understand that your coach wants to win, all the criticism makes more sense. This doesn't mean every statement from your coach will be directed to winning while in practice or games, but the main criticisms will come from a place of wanting improved performance that leads to winning. Take those points in and work to improve as you get coaching criticism. The night after a game probably isn't the time to work on things, but as you get back to practice you can use coaching to help guide your practice focus for improvement.

Chapter Four: What is My Coach Looking For?

If they aren't talking to you, you need to talk to them.

All coaches have different personalities. Many coaches are very outgoing and direct with coaching and will give feedback constantly. Others are more reserved and may be taking more mental notes than verbal coaching. If your coach isn't talking to you and you are craving more coaching, bring an instance of your failure to the coach and ask how to improve that part of your game. Sometimes the best advice and coaching comes from times when players seek help.

No coach is perfect.

Just like you, coaches make mistakes. Although coaches are unlikely to admit fault in all instances (there are many, many reasons for this), your coach will sometimes not have an answer or may give a coaching tip that doesn't work. The key in these instances is to give your coach's advice serious consideration and work. This means days, or even weeks of effort using the coach's advice. If you aren't seeing improvement after giving real effort to the advice, talk to the coach. Make sure to explain your effort and talk through your difficulties. Remember, your coach's ego is tied to his coaching. Take an intelligent and respectful approach when talking to your coach about the things you are working on. Most times, you can come up with a plan that will help you by communicating with the coach in this way and he will trust you for giving his advice effort and then communicating with him about positive or negative effects from the coaching.

Some coaches don't want to hear from you.

Unfortunately, there are coaches who only want you to play for them and keep your mouth shut, always, unless it is to talk on the field about outs or strategy. You will know if you have this type of coach quickly, as they will accept no feedback from players and will likely cut player conversations off quickly.

They may yell at players and berate them, and many players find these types of coaches extremely difficult to play for. This type of coach doesn't mean you should pack up and quit. If this type of coach gives you coaching, your answer is always "yes coach." Give the coaching an effort, but the reality of these coaches is that they very rarely take the time to watch for technique changes. The good news is that not all coaches are like this, and if you can make an honest effort to get along well with this coach, it will help you greatly throughout your life when you have a boss or coworker who works this same way.

Read the room before going in.

One major tip for players, and one I use as a coach, is to read the room before you enter. If your coach is in a bad mood, act accordingly and don't make the situation worse by acting silly. If you have a great relationship with a coach, sometimes you can help them out by noticing their mood and asking about it. Coaches are people, just like you, and they appreciate when they are noticed. Simply talking to your coach about their feelings, when appropriate, can really help you to build a better relationship with your coach and the better the relationship with your coaches, the better coaching you receive from them.

Praise is great, and temporary.

Occasionally, you may receive praise for a job well done from your coach. When this happens, this praise shouldn't linger for longer than a few minutes. You aren't playing the game for praise from your coach, you're playing to get better and help your teammates to win games. Allowing praise to linger too long will keep you from continuing to strive for improvement. Praise should be short-lived, and so should negative feedback. Negative feedback, which accounts for most of the feedback you will get, stings at times. Take the emotion out of the message as quickly as possible and use the content to help yourself to positively impact your team.

Chapter Four: What is My Coach Looking For?

The structure of a team means that you will be playing together with a coach or several coaches as the directors of the team. You won't always have coaches you agree with, but you should work with your coaches as much as possible to help them to help you by remaining open minded and optimistic toward improvement. Arguing with your coach, talking to teammates negatively about them, or ignoring them completely are sure-fire ways to hurt your chances of playing and helping your team. If you feel you might say or do something that is going to anger your coach, try your best to keep it to yourself and remember that your coach wants to win. If you can find an appropriate time to talk with your coach, strike up a conversation about something non-baseball related. Many times, you'll find some similarities between you that can help when times get tough between you. I made all the mistakes in the book as a player when talking with my coaches. You don't need to make those mistakes, so start to look at the feedback you're getting as positive, in some way, for your career. And remember, the coach's favorite player is the best player, so get out there and work on your game!

This is the end of section one. You likely have more questions for yourself, but many of those answers will fall into place as you talk with your coach and take the steps to work your way onto the baseball team. It is important that you stay consistent with your attendance and effort in practice and games. If you have something going on in your personal life that isn't allowing you to be at every game, talk to your coach about it. The same goes for any advice you may need in school or with friends. Your coach is there to help you and if they are unable to, speak to your high school counselor or a teacher.

Section II: Training for Your Opportunity

Chapter Five: Get into a Routine

The main difference between baseball before high school and after high school begins is scheduling. Unless you have played on a highly organized travel team with set practice and play days, or on a middle school team, this may be the first time you will have consistent practices on multiple days each week, in addition to games. At the same time, you may have more homework, more events with friends, and clubs you're involved with. The key to managing the increase in activities is to start to develop a routine. This may take a couple tries to get right, but a good daily routine can be career and life changing in a very positive way.

What is a routine?

NOUN
a sequence of actions regularly followed; a fixed program. In a sentence: "I settled down into a routine of work and sleep"

A routine is the framework for some action you are performing. A very common daily routine for most Americans is to wake up, brush teeth, then get dressed. A routine can be a simple set of things you are going to do before you leave the house, or a more complex list based on the nature of the task and user. For instance, the routine for starting my car is to put my foot on the brake and press the 'on' button, but the routine for an astronaut is a series of switches, calls back and forth with ground control, and safety protocols to ensure the trip goes smoothly. For baseball purposes, routines should be realistic in both the time and effort required to finish the routine. Since the hours in a day are limited and there are many uncontrollable factors, a routine must be adaptable and simple, yet provide the essentials to boost your performance in both the short and long-term.

Why do you need a routine?

When those uncontrollable factors arise, madness has the possibility to ensue. I'm talking weather, schedule, umpire, coach, teammates, injuries, and any other type of oddity that could come your way. If you are in a weather delay and you went through a warm-up program before the game, but it was throwing some random amount, you are going to find it harder to do the right amount of warm-up to use the second time before the game starts again. Injury and performance issues become more likely in a scenario like this one, but by using a routine you will be able to track your throwing easier and restart knowing how much more you are able to handle to get ready to play again. You need a routine because your health, continued development as a baseball player, development as a person, and performance all depend on it.

Does every player need a routine?

You need a routine whether you are a player, coach, or parent, period. Again, the routine doesn't necessarily need to be complicated. The whole point of the routine is to give you some structure so you can become the best version of yourself. For some players, some things may be a weekly routine, while others are done daily. Without a routine, you are at the mercy of luck and circumstance. With a routine, you take some control over your day and start making your own luck.

Chapter Five: Get into a Routine

How to start developing a routine.

Start by looking at your goals and assess the current state of your game. If you are lacking in body strength, speed, or agility write that down. If you want more arm strength write that down. If you are dealing with a sore shoulder or elbow all the time, write that down. If you stink at the backhand play, write that down. Any part of your game that you want to improve should be written down first. Once you have that, you can separate all those things into one of 3 buckets: body, hitting, or defense. There is a fourth bucket in routine, mental, but that is important on its own and so individualized that I'll make mental routine its own section. Once you have your tasks to work on, separated into your three categories, it is time to move to the action.

How to use a routine:

Start with the body

Since baseball does include movement with your body, your routine should start with the body work you are looking to improve. If you are trying to gain or lose weight, the routine may start with a weigh in then continue with monitoring food intake as well as exercise to nail your goals. If you have a sore joint or muscle, your routine should set aside the appropriate time to either rehabilitate or get that part of your body ready for practice or play. If speed or agility are issues, work on those immediately. Sprints, cutting drills, or reaction work should all be done hours before competitions or practices while your body is fresh. Off-days are a fantastic time to do a little extra work on your body. Working on your body takes motivation and I would recommend an accountability partner for this, because there will be many days where the bed feels nice and hill sprints don't sound appealing. Try things that you feel will benefit your body and start to add or subtract as you like. 15 minutes before your game starts is not the time to try and go through a complicated routine to get yourself healthy and ready for a game, it should be well in advance of that. The body routine will evolve as your body changes in what it needs and how you feel. A simple routine for youth players could be a dynamic warm up in the living room (plenty of these on YouTube) before going to the game so there is a foundation for a routine as the player gets older.

Offense or defense next, whichever is available.

Your routine shouldn't be exhausting, so whether you want to do defense or offense first shouldn't matter. For **offense**, your routine should cover the goals you are currently working on. This may be a couple of hitting drills or something else you feel is necessary to get you ready for the game. One key with your offensive routine is that it needs to work if you don't have any specialized equipment or space for whatever reason. The reasons for this are bus drivers take wrong turns and get to stadiums late, the weather may not allow any practice outside, or the pitching machine may break. At the pro level, we have many players who love to see velocity at the highest level possible as a routine, but if something happens and they can't get swings on that velocity before game time there are other options using whiffle balls, high-tee drills, or something to give them the work they still need. Offensive routines should be an appropriate length, although some players take more swings than others. Remember, for a routine you are looking at tiny improvement every day, not landmark moments. A routine should be short enough to make you want to do a little more, but long enough that you feel locked in for the game. Don't fall into the trap of swinging to swing and calling it a hitting routine. If you can't repeat it every day, it isn't a routine.

Just like your offense routine, your **defense** routine absolutely <u>should not</u> fatigue you to the point of lessened performance. Take time to go through the targets you have set for yourself on the areas you saw for improvement. There are plenty of fielding drills that can be found on Twitter or

Instagram to suit your needs. I like the hashtag #fridayfielders on Twitter when searching for defensive drills for infielders. Defense is important for all positions so find a few things to get you ready each day and commit to doing those things every single day to get ready for practice or competition.

All-told, a normal routine for a high school player could look something like this:

6:00 AM – Morning lift/agility work before school. Arm care with Jaeger bands or other implements completed at beginning of workout.

7:30 AM – Whatever time schools keep you before games – Class

Immediately upon getting to field – go through all exercises that may be specific to you that aren't in team stretch/agility. Then 5-10 minutes of hitting prep followed by 5-10 fielding prep. You should be able to complete all team exercises while still completing your routine.

After game or practice – Night lift if you didn't in the morning and include arm care into workout at beginning or end. Reflect on the game or practice. Write out a plan for the next day. Give yourself some affirmations, then go to sleep early enough so you can sleep 8-9 hours before your next day.

All day – eat foods that reflect your goals

How do I know if my routine is the right one?

Your routine won't be perfect at the beginning. You may over-plan and not have enough time or under-plan and be unprepared. Just tinker with the routine until it fits and gives you what you need. Most, if not all, of your other teammates will spend time in the dugout talking or on the field laughing about class and chatting about girls during the times where you will be preparing your body for long-term success. If you are standing out because of extra effort, so what? If you are a good leader on your team, you may persuade other teammates to take charge in their careers, which will only help your team get better. Don't stress about being perfect with your routine, just start with a couple of things, do them every day, and see how it goes.

What about in-practice or in-game routines?

Routines before pitches and between repetitions are also important to many professional players. The purpose of these routines is to enhance focus on the pitch, then relax that focus between pitches before the next pitch. Most of the swings you see between pitches are developed from work in practice and organically work into the game. Defenders will use communication between pitches or look to a different spot on the field to reset the vision for the next pitch. On deck routines often develop from years of observation as well. Although you will see players move a bat around and take some swings, the on-deck circle is typically a place of observation and the final spot to match to the pitcher's rhythm before getting into the batters-box. There is no perfect routine in the batters-box, but the earlier you come up with something you can do before and after every pitch the closer you will be to more consistent production as a player.

Lastly, and probably most importantly...

Your **mental routine** can help you to get into a great position to succeed without even taking a swing or rep. Physical routines are excellent ways to get your body locked in, but the body follows the brain. A mental routine starts with the first things you tell yourself and think about in the morning and ends with the last things you think about and tell yourself before you go to sleep. Highly engaged players use their minds to apply intense focus to practice reps, so the game reps are easier. There are a few books I highly recommend for players looking to gain the mental edge: **Heads Up Baseball**, by Ken Ravizza, **Mental Conditioning for Baseball**, by Brian Cain, **The Mental Game of Baseball**, by Harvey Dorfman, and **Mind Gym**, by Gary Mack. I read Mind Gym in high school and this book changed my entire mental outlook on play and practice. All of these books are great options but learning about the mental game won't do anything unless you take action and use the techniques you read about in the books. They're very helpful and learning to channel your brain toward your goals will improve your performance over the long-term.

To sum up routine:

When watching games on TV as a young child, I remember hearing how a certain player 'made all the routine plays' and thinking that nothing was a 'routine play' to me. Although every play is different, plays in games certainly do become easier as you implement specific things into your own routine. Don't wait until college for a coach to teach you a routine. Start to come up with one on your own, now. It doesn't have to be perfect, but you can always make some minor changes to the routine and find what works for you. Some of the greatest MLB players credit parts of their daily hitting routine to a drill learned in rookie or A ball. Some players will take a drill they like and use that drill every single day for the rest of their careers. Take that kind of intentionality to your game and see where your routine can take your career.

One Last Note on Routine

The higher your career climbs in terms of the level you play at, the more people who will have questioned your routine. One thing you must understand is that a coach who sees a player under-perform or struggle at any point will question the player's prep-work work first. If you are constantly asking yourself, "Why am I doing this?" about your routine, you should become more comfortable with explaining your routine. If your coach doesn't like your routine, ask what they would recommend and you should give it a try, but don't completely abandon something you've come up with and like. You can be coachable on your routine while still sticking to the process you've worked to develop.

Chapter Six: Strength Training

Two of the most common questions from young players to coaches are: How do I throw harder and how do I hit the ball farther? Typically, there are areas for improvement of both by improving body movement, but adding strength is an opportunity to improve as well. The main differences between high school, college, and professional games are the velocity and movement of the pitches, speed of the players, and bat speed of the hitters. At each level, the players are stronger. To take your next step upward as a baseball player, it might be a good time to train and improve your strength.

What is strength training?

Strength training is any type of training done with the purpose of improving your strength. Although I used strength training in the title, the needs of a baseball player run a bit deeper than that and you'll want to improve power, speed and agility, balance, mobility, and stability in addition to strength to optimize your body. When I say strength training for the rest of this chapter, I am talking about all of these facets of training from power to stability. A run-down of those below:
- Power is the amount of work done over a given period of time. The faster you move something, the more power you are using.

- Speed, in athletic terms, is typically referring to running speed. Strength and power are both crucial in developing speed as is sprint training. Agility is the ability to make dynamic movements in the response to a stimulus (like a batted ball).
- Balance includes several different facets, but to put it simply would be your body's ability to return the center of mass to a point that allows a return to stability (not falling over).
- Mobility is the ability to move your joints through a wide range of motion.
- Stability is the ability of your muscles and connective tissue to hold a joint at a certain angle or position to prohibit or allow efficient movement of other body parts.

When should you start strength training?

This is perhaps the most controversial portion of athletic development. Strength training could begin at any point once a person is able to walk and coordinate movements. Although urban legend says strength training at young ages could stunt growth, this has been largely disproven. Strength training through body-weight movements is a good idea for youngsters, but now that you're in high school it is time to get started if you haven't already. Although strength training can be done with body weight alone, the greatest gains can be found through overload and this likely means using machines, bands, or weights for resistance training. My general recommendation for beginning strength training using resistance goes like this:

Chapter Six: Strength Training

Freshman Fall:

Learn the basic movements for strength training. If you haven't started training using your body weight with pushups, sit-ups, pull ups, squats, and lunges - start ASAP. Some of the basics you should learn are: the goblet squat, front and back squat, RDL, deadlift, lat pulldown, bent row, bench press, incline press, shoulder press, and reverse fly. Each of these exercises have specific cues and techniques and you can search for them on YouTube. The amount of weight you lift should be light and is not important while you start learning the movements. This is also a good time to learn about plyometrics, which is essentially jump training as well as working on sprint speed and technique. You won't have a training routine yet, but hopefully you are starting to lay the groundwork for one by working on your weight training technique as well as sprint work two times a week each, or more if desired.

Freshman Spring:

If you took the time to learn to properly lift weights in the first semester of your freshman year, the spring during the season is a great time to learn to train during the season as well as beginning some mobility work. Hip, spinal, and ankle mobility are all crucial for building your body in a way that allows you to rotate effectively when you throw and hit. For your first spring, try different schedules like exercising before school and after school to see how your body reacts best. Again, YouTube is a great resource.

Sophomore to Junior Year:

Now is the time to look to build your body. Although some are late bloomers, if you work consistently in the weight room it will pay off for you. I recommend splitting the year up into different phases by using periodization or optimum performance training, so you are working to somewhat of a peak in the middle or end of your season with your body. If you are not getting great exposure during high school because of playing time or poor competition and you rely on tournaments or showcases for recruitment, try to peak during those months. Your body is going to see rapid improvement and quick recovery, so take advantage by training often and consistently.

Senior Year:

By this point, you should be extremely knowledgeable about weightlifting and planning your workouts. Continue to use a schedule throughout the year to peak at the right time and this is also a great time to give back and help freshman or sophomores who are in your shoes. Hopefully you have kept your focus on training to improve at baseball and continued to use a mobility, plyometric, and power focused training program. This base of training and the habits learned will serve you well as you transition to college or professional baseball.

How to train?

In the previous section, I mentioned some topics such as: periodization, optimum performance training, weightlifting, plyometrics, and mobility. A quick YouTube or Google search can give you answers for each of these, but you can typically find resources from your physical education teachers on campus as well. Baseball players are sometimes told to keep weight training to a minimum to stay flexible, but in my experience, weightlifting can be a positive aide to mobility, especially when coupled with mobility specific training. One additional important subject, when discussing training, is nutrition. Learning to eat and refuel your body after practices and games is extremely important. As you move through high school, it is important to manage your body composition (essentially body fat percentage), so you maintain your health. Excess body fat will hinder your performance just as bad, if not worse, than very low body weight. Consistently maintaining a body fat percentage between 10 and 20 should always be the goal. Most local gyms will test body fat percentages free of charge and you can use a phone app like MyFitnessPal to track your food intake.

Many people do not have a gym at home and will be forced to go elsewhere to train. Gyms can get pricey, although there are cheaper options if you look hard enough. My introduction into weightlifting started by asking the football coach if I could lift weights with the football team early in the morning during the summer to learn how to do it. Although I was smaller and weaker than most of the players, I learned proper technique and best of all, it was free to do so. Ask your coach at your high school if you can do something similar to what I did and I bet you'll be in the weight room in no time.

Who to train with?

Once you establish the basics of movement and are getting into a routine, you might want to look for a partner. There are a couple friends who will be more influential than the rest when it comes to your development as a player in high school: your hitting partner and your workout partners. I would choose these partners wisely, although you may not have a wide selection to pick from. Good gym partners have the same goals as you, are similar in strength to you, and are focused on improvement in the weight room. Bad gym partners are distracting in the weight room, don't care about your goals, and are likely uncommitted to improvement. You want to find somebody who will be mad at you for slacking and will also celebrate with you when you succeed. Ideally, you can find a baseball player to train with at your school, but I've been in situations where it isn't possible to find a likeminded teammate to lift weights with. A partner isn't essential, but if you can find one, they can help you to stay accountable to a workout routine and push you when you don't feel like you have anything left in the tank.

Lastly, a few tips for the programming of your training. In general, you want to use roughly 2 times as many pull exercises (using the posterior muscles of your back, glutes, hamstrings etc.) as push exercises in your programming. Targeted core work can help with endurance, but the best ab and core exercise is lifting heavy weight, which you should take your time to work up to. The glutes, hamstrings, and lats should be targeted often in your workout routine. Over-developed quads, biceps, or pecs could lead to issues with running or throwing. If you have medicine balls available to you, rotational medicine ball throws can really aid to your rotational power. The key with these is to use a ball that is on the lighter, rather than the heavier side.

When you gain more strength, you may be tempted to look into supplements to improve your development. Strength training is a long-term activity that requires discipline. Eating properly and hydrating should be enough to fuel your body without any extra substances. When it comes to strength training, **do a little a lot rather than training in long sessions infrequently**. Light training every day is preferred to extremely hard, soreness inducing training a couple times a week. Start taking care of your body now, and it will thank you in the future.

Monday	Tuesday	Wednesday	Thursday	Friday	Saturday	Sunday
Practice	Game Day	Practice	Game Day	Practice	Off	Off
Balance and Leg Focus with Core Work	Upper Body Pull Focus and Plyometrics	Full Body Stretch Day/Yoga	Full Body Weight Training Low to Medium Intensity	Upper Body Push Focus and Agility Work	High Intensity Sprint Training and Lower Half Pull	Active Recovery with Hike or Bike Ride

*Sample 1 Week Schedule

Chapter Seven: Hitting, Throwing, Defense

Although this book is dedicated to hitting, the other facets of baseball need to be practiced as well. As a hitter and position player your responsibility is to help to score and prevent runs. Practices with your high school team will probably include some defensive work, but that doesn't mean you don't need extra. Every player will have certain areas where they struggle more or less than others, and sometimes it is impossible to work on your specific needs within a team practice. For this reason, you will need to take matters into your own hands and practice to improve your weaknesses. One investment I highly recommend is a tripod to get video from your phone so you can review after practice or game. You can find decent tripods that will serve your needs for $20-30.

Start with throwing.

One of the best investments for yourself to improve your baseball performance is to stay consistent with your throwing program. Throwing often and consistently gives you the opportunity to work on accuracy, arm strength, and hand-eye coordination. Furthermore, since hitting has a rotational element to it, the rotation in throwing can improve your bat speed. Most importantly, throwing often and consistently reduces the chance of injury from overuse in a game or tournament. Arm injury is a major problem for players of any age, but during the developing years in high school it can prove to have a more negative impact than any other time in your development. The more consistent you are, the less risk you are taking for injury when you play.

Hopefully you have found a throwing partner with similar arm strength to yours. Always warm up before throwing and an arm care band routine is an excellent idea for your arm health. If you have had a significant amount of time off, start your throwing routine slowly and keep your effort level in your throws below maximal levels. After a couple weeks of throwing, you can begin throwing with increased effort. Take your time at the beginning of your routine to warm up slowly, then move farther and farther apart from your partner. Focus on throwing to your partner's chest with every throw, regardless of the distance. Once you feel you have completely warmed up, move to long toss, and throw the ball as high and as far as you can for 8 to 10 throws. After those, move your partner in 20 to 30 feet at a time and maintain the same effort level with your throws, but keep them on a line. For more information on a throwing routine, you can talk to your local college coach (email them) or look for a resource online like Jaeger Bands on YouTube. You can throw with this type of effort often (around 3 to 5 times per week) and on the other days of the week throw with lower effort if you'd like.

Throwing often and using long toss are the absolute best ways to keep your arm healthy and improve your throwing velocity. You can take a month or two off from throwing each year if you'd like, but you'll want to have at least a month of consistent throwing before you jump into a game, if possible. If you know you need to improve your arm strength and throwing velocity, time off isn't going to help. If you have any type of pain in your shoulder or elbow that continues to linger, see a trainer or physical therapist. Throwing will often lead to soreness when you've had a long layoff, but the goal is to get to a point where there is no soreness following practice or games after you've thrown consistently for several weeks or months.

Chapter Seven: Hitting, Throwing, Defense

Poor weather conditions or lack of a throwing partner are the two most common issues for those who are attempting to get into a consistent throwing routine. While these issues can be annoying, they shouldn't completely hold you back from training. If you have access to an indoor cage, you can practice your throwing and even long toss into the side of the net. If you don't have access, you can even buy a pop-up net to throw into. If funds are an issue, you can set up a mattress and throw into that. Stay resourceful so you can continue to work on your arm health. Without a healthy, strong, and accurate arm you'll have an extremely difficult time getting onto the field to show off your hitting.

Hitting is important, do it often.

Hitting a baseball is notoriously one of the most difficult things to do in sports. Hitting skill can erode if you go long periods of time without taking some swings. It isn't necessary to hit for 12 months a year, but if you are playing games at any point then you should have some practice hitting the baseball under your belt. Two main issues when getting started swinging a bat again after a long layoff are body soreness and blisters. Both soreness and blisters can be significant issues and you should take the necessary precautions so you can avoid injury.

As your body develops and you add strength, your recovery after exercise will change a bit. Soreness after long workouts, especially if you haven't been in a routine, can be expected. When you get back to hitting, try to keep the first couple of sessions shorter than you would normally hit. In addition, always warm up prior to hitting. Your hitting warm-up doesn't need to be too long or elaborate, but it is important to do something before you start taking swings.

| Bodyweight Squats | Walking Lunge with a Twist | Pronation/Supination with bat | Inchworm Stretch | Thread the needle stretch | Jump Lunges | Skater Hops |

*Sample Hitting Warm-Up

Over time, your warm-up should help you to add mobility and strength while also priming you to hit. If you are hitting to the point of exhaustion before you have built a base of endurance from several days or weeks of consistent hitting, you may be too sore to perform the following day. Furthermore, issues with blisters or tearing of the hands from extremely long hitting sessions can really set back your plans. Your hands are particularly important in hitting and you may deal with problems from practice or games from overuse or scraping the ground. Here are some ideas for hand care:

Treat all scrapes by flushing the wound out with water and peroxide immediately.

After the game, bandage with polysporin. Cover the scrape with a light bandage during the game if possible, as well to keep dirt out. An infection on your hand could be a very severe issue if left untreated or cared for improperly.

Work on your grip strength when you aren't playing.

The best way to do this for most is to hold onto something heavy with a farmer's carry or a static hold with a weight you struggle to hold longer than 30 seconds. For players who have experience weightlifting, pull-ups and deadlifts are great for grip strength as well.

Check on your hands frequently when practicing.

Although you might feel great with your body and want to keep hitting, if your hands are starting to get sore and you feel they might develop a blister, stop hitting for the day. Blisters typically develop at the beginning of the season when the hands aren't acclimated to the workload, or during the season if the hands aren't properly taken care of. A blister that tears can be a major nuisance, so avoid them if possible.

Take care of your calluses.

The buildup of skin from the friction of hitting builds a callus. Although some buildup is a good thing to toughen the skin, if the callus is raised it could catch during the swing and cause a tear in the hands. A callus scraper is a great investment for every hitter.

Moisturize your hands.

Dry and cracking hands are sure to lead to issues. Keep your hands moisturized with frequent petroleum jelly or cream on your hands. Water-based lotions may leave your hands in worse shape, so get something that will hydrate your skin like a cream.

Wear batting gloves when you hit.

This is a preference for each hitter, but if you have blister issues, give batting gloves a shot. If you do use batting gloves, take care of them and when they begin to get dry you can add a bit of petroleum jelly to them to regain their suppleness. If they are tearing quickly, try a different batting glove type. If you get them dirty, clean them as dirt will break them down faster.

Use a different type of grip or tape on your bat if you are getting blisters.

Also, make sure grips are evenly distributed on the handle. An uneven batting grip could add undue pressure to the hands and lead to tearing.

No matter what you do, occasionally you may get a blister or tear your hands.

When this happens, keep the blisters clean and dry. Wrap your hand with a bandage and tape if needed. There are various products or remedies to try, but in my own experience I never did find something I liked enough to recommend to other people.

Only you will know the perfect amount of hitting and the perfect schedule for you throughout the year. I encourage all players to hit in stages from tee → flips → batting practice → machine work → game. If you are two weeks from playing, tee work for a couple days is a good idea before progressing to a couple days of flips before BP and finally machine work. If you are playing a different sport, tee work once to twice a week can be a great way to maintain some skills but taking 1-2 months completely off swinging a year, if you are staying active with another sport or vigorous exercise, can be a great idea. Some hitters hit 5-6 times a week for 12 months a year with very few breaks. If that works for you, there are no rules saying you can't train nearly every day. Try to choose a schedule you can stay consistent with and add to it as you go.

Practice hitting with intent to improve on something specific. After a long layoff, the intent can simply be to get your body moving again to get ready for future practice and games. However, as you get your body to a point where you have the endurance for more swings in a session, begin to focus on a specific part of your game. Whether that focus is to improve a specific mechanical piece, hone your approach, or improve bat speed, you should have a goal for your hitting session. I'll touch on intent later in this chapter.

Don't neglect the defense.

Staying consistent with your throwing and hitting routine is a great way to build your skillset. Applying that skillset to the game will mean you will also be responsible for playing

Chapter Seven: Hitting, Throwing, Defense

defense as well as hitting unless you are the designated hitter. As a defender your position falls into one of three categories: outfield, infield, or catching (not including pitching). You should do your best to train your defensive play whenever possible. You may have a secondary position that you will want to train as well, so adding a couple of days per week of defense is a great idea.

One issue with practicing defense is the lack of private time to work on improving fundamentals. If you can, take some ground or fly balls and get them on video. Compare great defenders to your own movements on the field to find areas for improvement. You may find some difficulty in pinpointing everything, so compare the videos and look to get better at just one little thing at a time. You don't need a full field or an experienced coach to help you practice your defense. Stay resourceful and work on parts of your defense so you are better equipped for practice and games.

Catchers have a special set of needs, so they should implement a few more parts to training. Mobility training was mentioned earlier in the book and it is important for all players, but extremely important for catchers. Hip and ankle mobility can limit the function of a catcher behind the plate. In addition to extra mobility training, catchers can train similar to the same way as other positions by getting video of receiving and blocking and working to make adjustments to improve technique and performance. If you can find pitchers who need to throw throughout the year, volunteer yourself for bullpens or live at-bats. Catching takes a lot of work, but good receiving and blocking can make you an impact player on your team.

If you pitch in addition to playing a position, do your best to keep your arm healthy. There are going to be times where teams may ask you to throw for them during the high school offseason. If you are ready to pitch and have been throwing frequently, there shouldn't be an issue with a couple innings to get extra work. However, if you haven't been throwing and aren't ready, you should refuse the invitation for your own safety and arm health. I'll talk about showcases and tournaments later in the book and hopefully clear up some of the questions about playing games with the goal of college recruitment.

Most importantly for training, get intentional with your reps.

A couple years ago, I read this fantastic book named <u>Grit</u>, by Angela Duckworth. In the book, Angela clears the air on what separates high achievers from the average. Although many have a head start in life due to circumstance or ability, this head start is not certain to lead to high-level achievement. In the book, Duckworth explains that it is through purposeful practice that individuals truly separate themselves from the average. Those who get intentional about practice see greater success.

So far in my coaching journey, I have worked with 8–10-year-olds who are extremely gifted, professional hitters who were late bloomers, and everybody in between. I have also seen intentionality at work and the impact it can have on improvement over the long-term.

For players who aren't intentional about practice reps, practices are mindless events where success either happens, or doesn't happen. Purposeless practices would be something like a pilot leaving the runway with the goal of landing somewhere, but not really concerned with the destination. Without consideration for the amount of fuel in the plane, this sort of flying could be very dangerous, and I don't know about you, but I'm not going to sign up for a flight that doesn't tell me we will safely reach a destination.

For players who are intentional with practice reps, there is a clear and defined goal or thought for the practice session. Whether this thought revolves around execution, mechanics, or training intensity depends on the current focus for the player, but individuals who take an intentional approach to practice reps are able to realize intentional gains. Not only are gains great for your performance, but they are mentally and emotionally satisfying. The intentionality of practice for many professional players is a positive feedback cycle that actually makes these players want to practice more.

In a recent encounter with the parent of a 14-year-old, the parent explained to me that his son doesn't, *"Put a lot of thought into his swings yet, because he is just a kid."* Later the same day, I worked with an 11-year-old who told me, "**I do every practice rep perfectly, so I get better. If it isn't perfect, I practice until it is.**" I found the contrast striking and the improvement of each has very closely matched the intentionality they display in practice reps (the 11-year-old has seen amazing improvement, 14-year-old not so much).

There is no perfect age to get intentional about your reps. If you are a player and reading this, you're probably pretty interested in your growth already and maybe don't understand how to get intentional. If you are a coach or parent, you may be banging your head against the wall attempting to see intentionality from your players.

For players:

Get all distractions out of your consciousness. Conversations end when you step into your practice environment. With every rep, keep your intense focus on improving the thing you set your sights on improving. It may even help to write in a journal and jot that thing down so that you can come back to the journal and note your development for that day on that thing. If you want to have a group of people with you who are intensely focused during their reps, allow them to focus when they are practicing as well. Push each other and talk about what you were each working on and ask them if they made improvements.

For parents:

The best thing you can do is attempt to foster an environment for improvement. Rather than praise for success and negative feedback for failure, try to make statements like, "Those extra swings you took where you focused on driving the ball oppo are really paying off with those two shots to the opposite field." Statements of praise for effort create a nice feedback loop for players and they will likely begin to analyze their own efforts the same way over time. Obviously, the results matter so when defeats happen, rather than finding room for complaints or negative talk, help to provide a road map for improvement. Take notes on your child yourself and if mistakes are consistent, you can add valuable information the child may not be aware of like, "The last few weeks the curveball has given you trouble. Let's look at your swing to see if we can find something to fix that and mix up the pitches in batting practice to you so you get some extra reps on it." For a coach and parent, you can't make the players think or act a certain way, so your best efforts are to model the behavior you want and give feedback that sets the emphasis on the efforts of the players.

Whatever your circumstance and level of current intentionality in your practice routine, there is likely an area for you to improve your game by simply monitoring that area. Remember, you are interested in long-term gains when training, but will likely see short-term as well. If you find yourself overly critical or stressed, you can always switch gears to finding relaxation or calm in training and let your intentional focus guide you back to a more mellow mindset. Take control of your career by getting intentional with your reps, you won't regret it!

Chapter Eight: Games are Overrated

I'm going to start this chapter by saying, first and foremost, I love baseball games. I love to attend baseball games of all ages and especially loved playing in games when I was still able to. Baseball takes a different type of attention to the game to follow along and the action can be extremely exciting. With this said, playing in baseball games is not the best way to train to be better at playing baseball. As a means for getting better at baseball, games are overrated.

Training in most settings is all about efficiency. For instance, if I am working for a fast-food restaurant the manager will make sure I am trained to properly do the job in the shortest amount of time possible. The issue with sport training is it can be easy to forget about efficiency and assume the time to train is unlimited. Training for baseball, whether in the weight room or on the field, should also be geared toward efficiency. Playing a baseball game will take around 2-3 hours and players get 4-5 at-bats and maybe 4-5 defensive chances (more if catching). If you took the same amount of time and practiced hitting and defense, you could be looking at 150-200 swings and close to 100 defensive reps. Of course, the number of repetitions means less than the quality, but I'm making a point. Games are an inefficient way to train for baseball

There are too many reasons to begin to guess why so many are motivated to push children to play excessive games during the summer, fall, and winter months. I'm here to tell you that you can take a different path. Countries like Venezuela and the Dominican Republic have a very different system of player development for the youth. Many children in the Caribbean and Latin American nations play baseball through little league, and around 12-13 years old are recruited to play and go to school at an academy. These academies serve as high schools and training facilities for young players who are aspiring to sign professional contracts, which they are eligible to sign at 16 years old. Academy schedules may vary slightly, but most are on a 5-6 day per week schedule. During the time players are enlisted at an academy, they may play few or no games at all. The time each day is spent on developing tools to become more attractive to sign for professional teams.

The international model for player development probably doesn't work perfectly in the United States. It would be like sending a child to boarding school with hopes of signing a professional contract and a lower emphasis on education. However, I do believe there is a strong lesson to learn from baseball in other countries. Fewer games with more time to develop in training will give you a much better chance to become the player you're dreaming of becoming. Rather than letting your F.O.M.O. (fear of missing out) manipulate you into playing a ton of games all year, spend your time more efficiently and train.

You may have caught on, but I would much rather use the word "train" than the word "practice." When you tell yourself you are going to batting or infield training, the word choice alone drives more focus into the session. And remember, training is best done efficiently.

Finding somebody to help you with your training can be a difficult process. If you don't have a family member or friend with knowledge about baseball and coaching, you may feel inclined to look for somebody who provides private lessons. Lessons are not a necessary component to becoming a good player, but it is common for many players to seek advice from others and pay for coaching. Because of this, I wanted to provide a list of questions and concerns you should look at when deciding who you want to work with.

What is the coach's goal for you?

Although this question shouldn't be a major stumper, it can lead to some eye-opening answers that may tell you to look for a different coach. You want to find a coach who is looking to help you achieve your goals and mentor you to be a better person and player. If a coach is uncomfortable with the question or is promising you a 12-year MLB career, I would move to the next one.

What is the coach's background?

This question is important, not because it is important to work with a coach who has a hall of fame background, but to get an idea for the person you are working with. Sometimes, you'll come across those who have moved many times in recent months or years, and this can help you to ask follow-up questions and learn more about the coach. A coach may be good with little to no playing experience and may be terrible with a long pro career. You'll need to analyze content for yourself later.

What are your core beliefs for…?

Whether you're looking for hitting, defense, or pitching instruction you should ask for some core beliefs. This question is more so you have some knowledge going into the session so you can work together effectively as quickly as possible.

What are the types of players you've worked with in the past?

It is important that you're picking a coach that will match your needs. A coach who specializes in youth may not be well-suited for professional level hitters and vice versa. If the coach feels confident about helping you at your level and you want to give it a shot, there are no rules and there are many great coaches who can help players of all ages.

What type of schedule do you have available? Does the schedule stay consistent?

All coaches who provide private lessons will have various scheduling availabilities or issues. You want to make sure you are planning to schedule with somebody who can be reliable for the time you have available.

After you have answered these, you may have new questions. Private instructors may be plentiful or scarce in your area, but don't feel pressured to choose before talking to them. Your private instructor will serve the purpose of introducing concepts and a direction toward improvement, but all the work is still up to you. Lessons will likely challenge you to learn a new skill and move differently and it will be a challenge. In an ideal setting, you have ample time to work on the new move before playing in your next game. Whether it was the coach on your team, your parent, or a private hitting instructor, when somebody else approaches you with a new or improved way to swing the bat it takes a bit of effort and practice to apply the technique in a way so you will have future success.

To best apply lessons:

Start with the end in mind

Why are you making an adjustment to the way you are swinging the bat? You must know the answer to this question to apply it to your game and believe in your technique. Also, regardless of the change in technique, the goal for hitters must be to compete against the pitcher with the intent of winning the at-bat. Your goal in a game should always be success. However, your goal in training should be more focused on the technique and ways to achieve that in-game success.

Purposefully practice the new technique

Whether the adjustment is in the setup or the movement of the body during the swing, you must practice the technique before applying it to the game. If there has been a change in the setup or gather, find a mirror, and execute thousands of repetitions until you no longer need to think about the movement. If you were given a drill that solves your swing issue, practice the drill with the intent of perfectly executing the drill. If you had a thought or approach adjustment, continuously grind on that thought while you practice hitting. Start with an easy form of practice like tee work and progress to flips, batting practice, machine, high velocity machine, then the game. If the move breaks down at any point, go back to where you were able to do the move every time for a bit, then progress forward again. And practice the technique or drills daily. Your swing is like doing your math homework, but more fun. If you don't do your math homework, you'll end up coming to class the next day having forgotten what you did. The same goes for your swing so take the time to practice the techniques.

Stick to one thing

As you develop some of the movements seen in great hitters in the MLB, make sure you stick to the process of one piece at a time. It isn't fair to yourself to look at post-game video and to pick apart several different things and attempt to fix them all. Do one piece at a time and it is OK to pat yourself on the back from time to time as you see your swing improve.

One hour a week isn't enough

In my time working with all the players I have worked with, the best players put in the time and the effort to improve. We can accomplish great things in the hour a week we spend together, but you must put in the extra work each day to engrain the swing pattern. Take 15 minutes each day to work on your swing movement and, if you can, another 30 minutes to hit balls fed off a machine or thrown in batting practice. I can guarantee that 2 months of purposeful work on this type of schedule will lead to massive improvements in your game. Several years of it and you will find a way to lead your team, league, or state in offensive production.

Playing games is overrated

I wanted to hit this point one more time in this chapter, because I feel very strongly about it. Playing three or four games a weekend may seem like the fastest way to improve your game. I'm sorry, but that isn't the truth. There is value to playing games. After all, our end goal is to be a good player in game. However, playing games as your primary means of development is a fatal flaw for your career. Your development happens when you can take the time to put in many repetitions on a consistent basis. If you play one day a week, great! The other six should be development days with purposeful practice.

You can develop your own private spot

I don't include this section to minimize the importance of money or assume all people have the land to make it happen, but it is possible to create your own training area. A batting cage setup with machine could range around 3 to 4 thousand dollars. If you have a family member or trusted friend close, you may be able to split costs to make it happen. If you don't have the space or money, pop-up nets and tees are much cheaper. You don't need to pay big money to make a small private spot, but the return on your investment will be worth it.

And finally, give it time and *communicate*

No hitting coach has a magic wand to fix your swing in one session. On occasion, players do see rapid improvement from working with a hitting coach one time, but typically it takes practice and time for things to click. If you're unhappy with the product you received from the coach you don't need to go back to him or her, but if you aren't practicing the techniques outside of your time with the coach then you can't blame them if you aren't seeing your desired improvement. Give it time and put in some effort. If things seem to be stalling or after you've put in the work you haven't found greater success, communicate with your private coach so you can come up with a plan together. As coaches, we work for the players, so we rely on your feedback to best help you to achieve all of your goals in baseball.

My last note for this chapter is to return to the title of it and further clarify. Games are overrated for your development. However, your training should be to improve yourself for games. It is best to stick to as few coaching voices as possible to keep the path of your development clear. Conflicting views and styles from hiring multiple instructors could lead to worse, not better play. By spending much more time training than playing, you will likely develop a deeper understanding of yourself and passion for the work you are doing. In the following section, I am going to start talking about in-game strategies for success. The most important thing for your success in the game is confidence and intentional work on your game will give you real confidence. It isn't quick and may even take years to develop, but this confidence inside you will help propel you through difficulty and adversity. All those extra swings, throws, and ground balls will pay off.

Section III: Shining When the Spotlight is On

Chapter Nine: You're the Best

There's only one place to start when talking about in-game performance...with YOU. When you're in the box, there are many factors outside of your control (weather, field, pitcher, umpire, defensive positioning, etc.). There is one main factor within your control: your mind. I've touched on some training ideas for your mind in the previous section of this book, but when the game is on the line it is time to perform. The best chance you have to succeed on the field is to have supreme confidence in yourself and focus on the task at hand.

In my time watching baseball, I've heard coaches attempt to coach confidence into the players before or during the game. Confidence takes longer than a pep talk, unfortunately. When I was a young player, I heard, "You need to play with confidence" about a billion times. I struggled to grasp the idea of confidence as a young player until somewhere around the middle of my high school playing career. During those moments, I was far from confident outside of baseball, but on the field I felt right at home and very confident. For you to discover your confidence on the field, start putting the work in and training yourself to be confident.

What is confidence?

The Webster definition is, "a feeling or consciousness of one's powers or of reliance on one's circumstances," or, "faith or belief that one will act in a right, proper, or effective way." Simply put, you are in the moment and participating without any distracting thought with a belief that you're doing the right thing. With confidence, you are like a lion hunting for prey. Without it, you are *powerless* and cowering in the face of competition.

How do I become confident?

That's the million-dollar question. The real answer: it depends. It depends on who you are, how you see the world, and the factors that are going into your confidence or lack thereof. If I had the solution to help nearly 8 billion people on this planet to become confident in everything they do, I'd surely let everybody know and we would probably have a safer and more harmonious planet to live on. Heck, if I could even teach myself to be confident in all situations, I would do it. The truth is that there are times when you are going to feel great and feel confident in yourself and your abilities. There are other times when you are going to feel like curling up in a ball and quitting right there. In both times we forge on and do the best we can!

Strategies for confidence:

One turning point for me in my confidence as a ballplayer was a great book I mentioned earlier called <u>Mind Gym</u>, written by Gary Mack. At the time of reading the book I was afraid of just about everything in the game of baseball. At one point in the book, the author details Michael Jordan's strategy for fear. Jordan, instead of cowering when he was afraid, changed the fear into anger. He used this anger to drive through the fear of failure. While this strategy was a great one for me for a period, it is not the only strategy. Other strategies include: choosing an alter-ego like a superhero to see yourself as during competition, meditation about the person you'd like to be and you will see yourself as during competition, visualization of success before the game starts, reminding yourself during the game that failure is very minor and baseball is only part of your life, staying process-oriented during the game, and positive self-talk. For many players, affirmations (I worked hard today, I love myself, I am a great player etc.) before bedtime can help to close the book on the day and build for the next.

One thing guaranteed to build confidence:

One thing mentioned in a previous chapter that may be the best thing for building confidence...work. If you put the work in and you continue to put the work in day after day, your time in competition begins to feel more like an earned right as opposed to an uncertain assignment. The more purposeful practice you employ in baseball and the training of your body, the easier it is to feel deserving of each at-bat and ground ball. The best athletes in the world work all day to hone their craft. It is work to wake up at a certain time to train their bodies, work to eat the right food during the day, work to rehab injuries and prepare for competition, work to improve their baseball technique, work to talk with reporters after the game regardless of how good or bad the performance was, and work to get a good night's rest before waking up and doing it all over again. All of this work can give the impression that sports aren't fun. The truth is that most of these things *aren't work* for athletes. Sport is fun and it is exciting to work on the thing that they are truly passionate for. And a lot of these things are fun as well. Much of the work happens with other people and teammates around so there is a group element that can make things fun. Some of the work is in the shadows and no other people will know about the struggle and effort it took. All this work adds up and builds confidence.

The first step in becoming a great performer is to take this overwhelming confidence into your competition. All the worry about yourself should be out of your mind and the only focus should be to win each opportunity you get. You are the best for each opportunity because you've done the hard work and have the will to be the best. Always take the mindset that you are the best in competition and work as hard as you can to build your skills while in training.

Chapter Ten: Planning for Success on Gameday

Once you've finally worked your way into a game, it is time to let your preparation show itself. Whether you are playing 1 or 7 days a week, each time you have the opportunity to hit you want to make the most of each at-bat you are given. The side sessions, workout routines, and practices are important for your preparation. Equally as important is your plan against the pitcher you are facing. In professional baseball, players have the luxury of scouting data to learn what a pitcher will bring to the table as well as video, but in most amateur levels you don't get this opportunity. This chapter is dedicated to the study and planning you should take for each pitcher you face. You don't need a complicated plan or to know every detail of the pitcher, but these characteristics are quick-study items before your at bats.

What is the pitcher's release window?

Simply put, where is his release point? Does he have a consistent arm angle, or does he change it based on the pitch he is throwing, or does he try to throw from different angles to trick hitters? The arm angle helps to tell you spin and the spin helps to tell you movement so study him as he throws when he is warming up to find his release point, so you can see the ball clearly.

What kind of stuff does he bring to the table?

Is he a high velocity or low velocity pitcher? Do his pitches move late, and which direction do they move? Does he change speeds well or rely on one speed? Checking velocity in the bullpen is difficult, but warmup pitches as well as the other hitters in your lineup can give you clues for your at-bat so you know what you should expect.

Where is he targeting?

Does he try to throw the ball away, in, high or low? Most pitchers want to throw it where they won't get hit, so this doesn't mean you need to chase his spot, but it can help you understand where he gets people out. If you think you can cheat a bit to hit his spot you can also do that from time to time for some big rewards.

How are your teammates reacting to his fastball?

If you have teammates in front of you who are typically on-time with an average fastball, watch how they react to the new pitcher. If they are late the pitcher may be deceptive and you may want to start your moves slightly early and if they are early you may want to start slightly late. You can also adjust your target to pull or opposite field based on how his fastball plays if you wish. One big mistake some hitters make is to think they will fare better than their peers with the same approach. Let your teammates failure teach you something so you don't need to fail to learn the adjustment for the following at-bat.

What pitch does he throw when he is in a jam?

My definition of a jam goes like this: Leadoff double or triple, runner in scoring position with less than two outs, bases loaded at any time, back-to-back extra base hits, or any other time your team has been fortunate enough to string 2 or 3 good at-bats together and put men on base. During these times, some pitchers will use a pitch or a pitch sequence they feel will get strikeouts or soft contact at a high rate. Many times, this sequence relies on the hitter taking one strike and swinging at one outside the strike zone. If you see this pattern, you may be able to sit on the pitch others would take and become the hero for your team. Other pitchers stick to the same pitches and sequences they use when they aren't in a jam, which is also great information for you to know for when you're hitting in one of these situations.

What sort of timing or rhythm does the pitcher use?

Does he have a high or short leg lift? Does he take a full or a short arm swing? Does he take a lot of time between pitches with runners on or does he work quickly? For many pitchers, they use the same consistent arm swing and leg lift during the game. Knowing this and establishing your rhythm to match his before you get to the plate is a major benefit to you. Occasionally, pitchers will change the leg lift and timing frequently. Although this can give some hitters trouble, if you know this going in you won't be surprised when it happens and using a condensed version of your load might help you out as well. Furthermore, you will be a better baserunner if you pick up on his timing before you get on base so you can help your team score more runs.

Can you eliminate one of his pitches?

The baseline arsenal for a college or high school pitcher usually includes a fastball, curveball or slider, and a changeup. If you know he doesn't throw one of these, you can eliminate it and now only must look for two pitches. If he can't land one of these pitches for strikes you can eliminate it as well. Lastly, if one is a pitch that will never fool you and you will see it and will be able to adjust to it early, you can eliminate that as well and react if you see it. Sometimes you can try to eliminate one of his pitches after watching him warm up in the bullpen or on the mound, but most often it will take a couple of hitters before you can figure out which pitch will not be a factor in the at-bat.

Does he have a consistent pattern?

Lastly, what is his pattern? I wrote this last, because you will not often find a pattern that will help you in the batter's box that is consistent over every type of situation. Most times, pitches are called by a coach at the amateur level so the pattern may come from the coach and can change based on the coach's observations, so you may sometimes pick up on the pattern. Knowing the pattern is a good thing if you can catch onto something, but I would put most of the emphasis on the previous categories and if you do run into a pattern, then great.

Like everything else in baseball, seeing these categories for analyzing pitchers may seem like a daunting task and one you might overthink. However, it takes a few pitches and very minimal thought to go through this entire list. There are other things to look for in a pitcher such as pitch tips and movement profiles, but this list is great way to approach your at-bats as a prepared hitter who has great odds for success. Your next goal should be to start formulating a plan of attack to win against the pitcher.

There are eleven ways (and probably more) to end an at-bat: sac bunt, sac fly, ground out, line out, fly out, walk, hit by pitch, catcher's interference, reach on error, reach on hit, or strikeout. Because the strikeout doesn't lead to any contact or in-game action, most hitters and coaches have a stronger reaction to strikeouts than any other type of out. In turn, many hitters work at-bats with the goal of 'not striking out' rather than 'hitting the ball.' It is this mindset that leads to reactive, rather than proactive hitting.

A reactive at-bat shows itself many ways, but one of the most common is something like this: fastball taken for strike one, fastball fouled away for strike two, off-speed pitch in the dirt swung at for strike three. A deeper dive into the thought process when these types of at-bats occur, in my experience with players, has revealed a plan for each pitch that possibly looks like this: was sitting on breaking ball first strike, thought he would throw breaking ball second strike but swung when pitcher threw fastball, thought pitcher was sticking to fastball for strike three. Another way a reactive plan manifests itself is like this: curveball in the dirt swung at for strike one, fastball down the middle taken for strike two, fastball high swung at for strike three. The plan for the second scenario typically plays out like this: was sitting fastball strike one, looked curveball strike two since pitcher started curveball, figured curveball was coming again strike three. These are only two scenarios that play out because the hitter is reacting to the pitcher's decisions, but there are many more.

Rather than reacting to the guy on the mound, begin to push the odds in your favor by playing the game on your terms. To be clear, this doesn't mean you should take the exact same plan to every situation for the rest of your career. To develop a plan that is going to work, you need to do a little bit of extra work and watch the game to figure out the best plan. Although planning fully for an at-bat should happen as the games and situations develop, often you can plan before the game and even the night before if you know the pitcher you are facing. Let's dive into the things you should be looking for.

You've already scouted the pitcher.

Figuring out your opponent's game is the first step in working to develop a plan. By knowing about the pitcher, you can use the rest of the information in the game to figure the best way to win your at-bat. If the pitcher offers a very hittable arsenal you may take a different plan to the plate than one who is going to make good contact more difficult.

What is the game situation?

When innings speed up for an offense and there are multiple hits, pitchers will sometimes work to slow the game down by changing the pitch arsenal. In bunting situations pitchers will sometimes rely on a certain pitch. Later in games, many pitchers will change the way they are working to either get more strikeouts or more balls in play, depending on the score. Hitting with first base open and a runner on second base will change the pitcher's plan as will the portion of the lineup they are facing.

Most importantly, what are your strengths?

The pitch arsenal and pitcher's plan are important, but you need to understand your strengths and stay realistic and optimistic for your own chances at the plate. Develop your plan accounting for: if you struggle heavily when you try to force the ball to the left or right side of the field, find a pitch type difficult or impossible to hit, or have a certain part of the strike zone you dominate. Scouting reports and team plans may be extremely helpful but sticking to your strengths is your best opportunity for success. Occasionally this may mean the matchup with the pitcher or situation is a tough matchup for you, but nothing is ever impossible. Hopefully your focus in training and practice is centered around growing your strengths so you aren't limited when the game comes, but there are plenty of situations in MLB history where the hitter had major limitations and still found success (Kirk Gibson's 1988 World Series homer comes to mind).

When deciding your attack plan, start with your goal for the at-bat. Is this an at-bat where you want to work for an extra-base hit (double, triple, homer), beat a defensive alignment, hit a ball into the outfield, move a runner, or simply move the ball forward (into play)? If you can't walk to the plate with this goal in mind, you can't start to plan for the at-bat. Knowing your strengths will help you to pick the best option to start with. If you want to:

Work for an extra-base hit:

You should be aware of your power and which parts of the strike zone you have your best chance at making this happen. If you don't feel comfortable hitting a ball into the right or left-center gap without an outfielder running under the ball, you may have one corner outfielder playing closer to the gap than the other which will leave you an opening. Generally, you are looking for a pitch to put your best swing on and you want to stick to that. If you go to the plate looking for an extra-base hit, you must be willing to give up the corners of the plate in most cases. When you get your pitch to drive, take your best swing and hit it slightly under center to keep it off the ground. Taking only this goal to the plate will probably leave you with more strikeouts and flyouts than you'd like, so pick your spots for this goal for times in games when the risk is worth the reward.

Beat the shift:

Defensive shifting in the MLB has become highly specialized to fit against certain players and situations, but high school and college shifting can be much more gut-driven and sometimes even careless. If you see a player out of position you can intentionally pick on that player for a nice reward for you and your team. Some common position issues I see are outfielders who are too deep, too shallow, wildly shifted to one side of the field or another, middle infielders shifted strongly into the holes or in the middle, and corner infielders playing excessively deep or off the line. It is difficult to intentionally work a ball to the strong side of the field on the ground between a corner and middle infielder if that section of the field is open, but openings in other areas can become easy to pick on. You may need to look for a pitch that allows you to work the ball to the area you want, but when working to beat the shift you should only attempt to do this if you can cover most of the strike zone to hit the ball to your desired area. If you are shifted to your pull side and you are a hitter who struggles to hit the ball to the opposite field and are also looking to hit the ball for an extra-base hit, you'll have to hit over the shift for success.

Hit the ball to the outfield:

Double plays are the second worst outcome of an at-bat, after a triple-play. Any time you have the opportunity to score a run with a ball in play but need to hit it to the outfielders to avoid a double-play you should stay committed to hitting the ball to the outfielders no matter what happens in the at-bat. There's no 'one size fits all' approach here and everybody is different in strengths, so work on your plan in practice for when this happens in the game. If you are unsure of your ability to hit the ball into the outfield, bunting for a hit in the direction of the weakest or slowest defender may be a great idea as well. If you already hit the ball to the outfield more than the infield, you may not need to make any drastic changes to your plan. I cannot stress enough that you will need to practice this for yourself before you are in the situation to help yourself succeed.

Move a runner:

When you need to move the runner (from first to second or second to third) you are going to need a selfless approach to the at-bat while sticking to your strengths. If you stink at hitting a ball on the ground between the first and second baseman, learn to drag or push bunt for that situation. I find that hitters who succeed in this situation can take the pitch in the middle to inside part of the plate to the opposite field (for a right-hander) if needed but will also avoid rolling-over on the outside pitch. In situations where your team is attempting to move runners you may be given a hit and run sign from your coach, so don't let this surprise you. Work on the skill of moving runners with a ground or fly ball often. If you are unable to pick up a hit, moving a runner can be extremely valuable to your team.

Move it forward:

Sometimes the chips are stacked against you. It may be the pitcher with a big arm, the umpire with a big zone, or some minor injury you must overcome to win the situation. When a 'win' in an at-bat is putting the ball in play, find a way to do it as early as possible. In most situations, you want to swing at pitches that you can hit well. However, in situations like this you will likely want to switch your focus to the pitches that the pitcher is throwing most often and look for that. Really good pitchers who are on top of their game are successful most often when they throw the fastball to a zone in the strike zone and are able to pair a deceptive off-speed pitch from the same zone, to start, that ends up a ball. If you are in 'move it forward' mode, you'll likely be fooled by that pair but stick to the plan. You're looking for the spot where he will throw the pitch and you probably aren't going to hit something for extra-bases, but that's the tradeoff you'll make for this type of win and it doesn't mean you won't end up with a single.

Work a walk:

I didn't include this above because it is not a valid goal for a hitter. At no point, ever, should the goal be a walk. As the late Hall of Famer, Hank Aaron, said, "The pitcher has got only a ball. I've got a bat. So, the percentage in weapons is in my favor and I let the fellow with the ball do the fretting." Attempting to walk gives the control you have of the at-bat away to the pitcher, and you must never give up control of the at-bat. Walks will occur because a pitcher cannot throw the ball over the strike zone. If you focus on your job of hitting to win the at-bat, you will force the pitcher to make mistakes and give you walks but you should always work to hit. Another element of control is your ability to work hit-by-pitches by holding your ground in the batter's box. When a pitcher knows you won't move when he throws inside, you may force him to throw the ball over the middle of the plate in the future.

So, what does a good plan look like?

Your plan, as stated earlier, should reflect the goal of the at-bat. When looking to do damage, the zone you swing at should generally be smaller than the zone you are looking for when simply looking for contact. If the velocity of the pitcher is not fast enough to require you to cheat to it, you have no reason to set your sights on one pitch or another...although you can always mildly guess based on your observations of the pitcher's pattern in each situation. You may not have any experience with pitching or catching, but you must remember that those two are working together to get you out. You may also have the opposing coach calling pitches to get you out. They are going to call pitches that they feel are going to get you out, so your reaction to a pitch has some influence on the subsequent pitch calls. If you take a pitch, that may give some reaction, but it can be difficult to gauge when a hitter takes a pitch because he can't hit it or because he was fooled.

A good plan chooses the appropriate amount of risk for the given situation. The smaller the zone you look for and less frequently the pitcher throws to the spot you're looking, the lower the chances you'll get that pitch. Again, you must know your strengths to decide if you're willing to wait a pitcher out for a certain spot because you can provide a big reward (hit) when you get that pitch, or if you're going to look more where he is throwing often so you get a couple chances in your at-bats for a ball you're looking for. Good plans are slightly flexible when you see the pitcher is taking a different plan than you thought in the at-bat, but if you throw your plan out after one pitch, it wasn't a good plan. If you are throwing your plan out frequently, you need to look at your process for planning and come up with different observations. World class hitters have world class plans. Although pitchers are trying to set hitters up to get out, the best hitters work to set the pitcher up by using all prior knowledge of the pitcher with the success the pitcher has had against that hitter. Learning to set a pitcher up takes many years of study, but by starting to plan now you can get on that road to mastery.

As Mike Tyson said, "Everybody has a plan until they get punched in the mouth." If you observe a pitcher in his warm-up pitches and he is unable to throw a certain pitch near the strike zone, you may want to cross that pitch off the list of pitches you are looking for. This simple strategy will help you to win some at-bats, but occasionally a pitcher will still have the ability to throw the pitch you crossed off your list. You're going to get out a lot in your baseball career, so a minor loss like this should be filed away in your mind. Don't give your plan up completely because the pitcher deviated from your estimate. The odds are in favor of those who stick to their plan and continue to work to refine the planning process.

Some things pitchers, catchers, and coaches look for when calling pitches.

I have heard of football coaches who will script the offensive plays to start a game to see how the defense reacts to those plays to adjust later. Baseball is typically more of a fluid situation regarding the calling of pitches and pitchers will react with each pitch to decide the next pitch. There is a bit of planning by pitchers, catchers, and coaches based on observations like: how far you set up from the plate, spot in the order, whether your swings are on time, your balance and posture during your swing, your past performance, your prior statistics, and even your body size. Ask your teammates for feedback on these things and even ask the pitchers, catchers, and coaches on your team where they would throw you. This can be helpful for your plan while you hit, but also for your targets while you practice. Many hitters are pitched with a mix of pitches in tougher spots based on the observations above, while others may get thrown more repeatable pitches. There's nothing wrong with getting some extra information about yourself so you can come up with a great plan to hit. This takes me to the final, and most important part of your plan.

Once again, confidence is king.

By bringing a plan to the plate, you are adding one extra layer of preparation to your game. Not only does preparation lead to better chances of success from a strategy standpoint, but it also adds to your confidence. You can fake confidence for one or two at-bats, or you can build real confidence through sweat-equity. All the time and effort you put into your game adds to your confidence when you are in competition. Those who have put in the work are able to return to a confident state quicker and maintain confidence longer. There is no measurement to confidence, or the energy confident individuals give off, but it adds to your team in many positive ways. Every post you read, swing you take, mental practice you do, and weight you lift adds to your momentum before you ever step foot into the batter's box. Start walking to the plate with a plan and learn to stick to it. Keep growing, keep learning, and give 'em hell!

Chapter Eleven: Show it Off

All your planning and effort you put into your abilities will put you in a position to be prepared for your opportunities in games. Although I'm not a proponent of playing an egregious number of games throughout the high-school offseason, it is important to remember that your training efforts are to be a better player when it is time to play in a game. You will notice improvements in games along the way, but you can expect to play games at about the same performance level where you train and practice. The nervousness and butterflies before a game may never completely go away, but the more prepared you are the more likely you are to feel calm and confident during the competition. Some of your teammates will have a complete change in personality and demeanor on game day, but if you train properly you can learn to stay more consistent with your behavior between training and games. Included in this chapter are some ideas for game day that will help you and your team in many ways.

Leave the eyewash for the others.

Your gameday schedule may vary depending on travel, weather, or school regulations. The schedule will allow you some time to get yourself ready with team stretching and throwing, but also a few minutes here and there for your own routine. If you have been working on things to improve your game consistently, you will have an idea for the things you can do to prepare you for the day's game. Your teammates who aren't taking the time and effort to improve themselves consistently may do things like excessive yelling, extra sprints, or stretching in front of parents and fans. It is best to do the things that get you ready to play and stick to those rather than doing things for attention. In fact, if your focus is on the attention you're receiving from others, you probably aren't in the best frame of mind to beat an opponent. You may have a slight change to your uniform on gameday such as adding an arm sleeve or eye black. Be yourself and if you like to do those sorts of things and your coach doesn't have any issues, go for it. Just keep the extra eye wash to a minimum and use the routine that has worked best for you when you're performing well in training.

Gameday is for the team.

All your training and practices should be to build your game up. When your team is playing, the script flips and you are now working solely to win the game as a team. If you aren't in the lineup you will still have things you can do to improve the team. Watch the other pitcher and share your observations. If you think there is a defensive weakness, tell somebody. Maybe you can pick up on the other team's signs, which can prove to be extremely helpful. At a minimum, your team will need a catcher to warm up the pitcher or somebody to warm up an outfielder between innings. Stay ready to help whenever possible. Be positive to your teammates coming off the field and stay supportive. Some of your teammates may want to talk about how they or you should be playing instead of sitting on the bench, but those aren't the teammates you want to follow. Gameday is a team day and if you aren't given the opportunity to hit or play defense as much as you'd like, work for that opportunity on those practice and training days.

Your coach is trying to win.

The strategy for the lineup and the signs given to the players who are hitting will be your coach's best effort to win the game. Coaches spend time planning and organizing thoughts to find the best chance to win. Your place on the team is to make yourself a standout because of your great play so you are in the lineup to help your team win. If you are very similar in skill to another on your team in your position, you may not see as much playing time as those who are greatly superior in ability or performance for that position. If you want to be a great player for your team, start by trusting your coach and leave the decisions to them. Your parents and other teammates may have things to say about the coach but do your best to stay out of those conversations because they will not help you to become the best player you can be.

Dominate the controllable.

Your preparation, your actions, and your responses are all within your control. By doing a great job with the things you can control, the things you can't control won't play as much of a factor. Umpires will always make bad calls and if you assume this will happen when you go into a game, you won't be surprised. Whenever you make a mistake, you must immediately move to the next moment and forget the incident. You will have plenty of time to think about the game and all the plays you had after the game, so stay in the present and keep striving to win each moment.

Get on base.

The one bit of hitting-specific advice I wanted to include with this chapter is: get on base. Of course, all players are trying to get on base when they play, but I also mean this as a figurative statement to do the task you're given when the opportunity comes. In the literal sense, there are times where players will avoid a hit-by-pitch because they "want to hit" or other times where players may swing at a ball out of the zone to avoid a walk. In competition, take every opportunity you are given without attempting to make it more than you're given. Take that hit-by-pitch or walk because it is going to help your team. On defense, make the simple play rather than overcomplicating an easy out. When you're given a sacrifice bunt sign put the bunt down well on the correct side of the field, then run as fast as you can. "Do your job" is another way to say "get on base." Do your job and your team will thank you and more opportunities for success will find you.

Playing time is earned.

I'm assuming, at this point, you've already started to understand this point, but it is important to bring it up again. You can earn your opportunity to play through proven performance in past practices and games. The goal should be to perform at a level that is so much better than your peers that the choice is easy for your coach. If you are performing at a similar level to others, occasionally the coach will decide to play the player who seems to work the hardest. If you feel you outwork a similar player to you, the key isn't that you need to show the coach you work harder. The key is that you need to perform better. This means improving your performance through training and showing it when you have opportunities in front of your coach at practice or games.

Have fun!

I didn't include this last in this chapter because I think it is the least important part of playing. Actually, I think having fun is as important as playing with confidence. You probably have high expectations for yourself and your performance, but while in the games you need to let go of those expectations. The sooner you are able to relax and focus on winning each opportunity, the more enjoyment you will have in games. Of course, winning is more fun than losing, but the game should be enjoyable regardless of outcome. You never know how many games you will get to play, so enjoy each time you have the uniform on and are playing with your teammates.

The following chapter will cover post-game and post-training reflection. In that chapter, I will cover journaling for hitters as a tool you can use during games to help you perform better. Keep the topics of this chapter in mind the next time you are in a game and the ideas in the following chapter will be there to help you progress and learn from your game and training experience.

Chapter Twelve: Reflect on Your Performance

Giving your best during the game means that you must keep your mind focused on the current play at all times during the game. If you lose focus and begin to think about the previous play, you will run into problems. Many players will play some of their best games while feeling ill because they are forced to keep attention to the present moment without allowing past frustration or success cloud judgement. Staying in the present isn't a hall pass to assume you always make perfect decisions and plays that don't require adjustment. To continue to advance your game you must reflect after a performance to find the areas where you need improvement.

Learning to reflect on performance isn't a skill you were born with, so it will be a learning process. The best way to reflect on performance is to stick to facts and throw emotion out of your analysis. For example, the facts of an at-bat could be the number of strikes, the pitcher, the pitch type, and the location of the pitch. Emotional responses would include statements like, "The umpire made a bad call," "I should have crushed that pitch," or "The pitcher got lucky." By sticking to facts, you can accurately determine your success or failure in each circumstance and find opportunity for improvement of your training or game process.

Reflection should be a routine behavior for after practices and games. It only takes a couple of minutes each day to reflect on an activity, but the value reflection provides can be far superior to any coaching you may receive. Reflection should be an activity where you shed light on room for growth as well as positive elements from the day. You can build optimism, which is belief that through effort tomorrow will be better than today, and organize your thoughts into realistic and actionable items for the following day. Take the extra few minutes after a competition, practice, or training session for reflection so you can keep working toward progress as a person and player. The following page contains an example of a daily reflection journal.

Daily Reflection

3 Things that went well:
1.
2.
3.

Areas for improvement:

Tasks for tomorrow:

Goal for tomorrow:

*Sample Daily Reflection

Since we are talking about journaling here, it is also a good time to talk about the benefits of starting a hitting journal. It is common to see college or MLB players walk back to the dugout after an at-bat and immediately pull out a journal to write something down. If you wait until the game is over, you may not be able to recall all the pitches in the at-bat and you may also miss some in-game patterns by the pitcher. In-game journaling should be brief but include enough information to help you during and after the game. In addition, you may face the same pitcher several times throughout the season or in your high school career so the journal can give you the advantage of extra information.

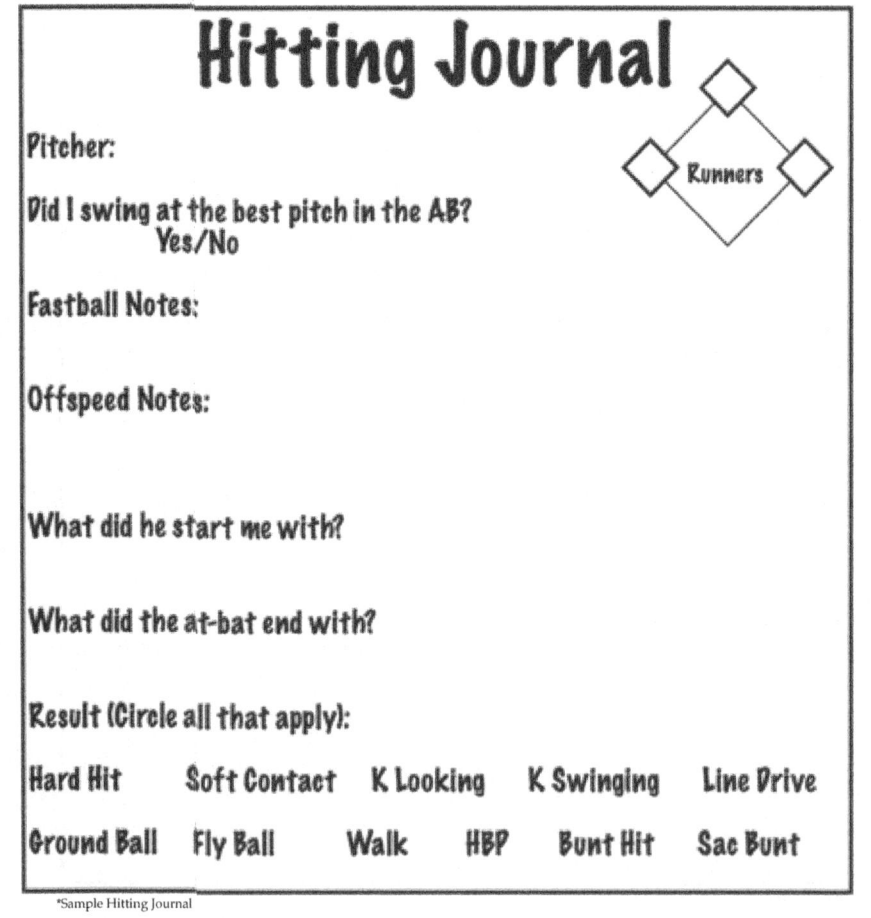

Hitting Journal

Pitcher:

Did I swing at the best pitch in the AB?
Yes/No

Fastball Notes:

Offspeed Notes:

What did he start me with?

What did the at-bat end with?

Result (Circle all that apply):

| Hard Hit | Soft Contact | K Looking | K Swinging | Line Drive |
| Ground Ball | Fly Ball | Walk | HBP | Bunt Hit | Sac Bunt |

Runners

*Sample Hitting Journal

When you spend time reflecting on your at-bats after games, it is important that you have a consistent barometer for success.

Chapter Twelve: Reflect on Your Performance

Hitting the ball well doesn't always guarantee a hit just as hitting it softly doesn't guarantee an out. As a hitter, you should look for markers that will lead to hits and success long term rather than grading at-bats based on the outcome of hit versus out. If you aren't getting hits, you might not be performing as poorly as you think, when looking at all the factors. Sometimes I'm amazed to hear how poorly a player is playing to then hear that he has hit the ball hard on a regular basis. If you're hitting it hard, that isn't a slump.

Start with defining success before you look at how successful you have been. For most, the definition of success should be hitting the ball hard consistently and being in a position to competitively play the game. If you aren't doing either of those, you may be in a patch that needs correcting. Video is a nice tool when looking at game performance, but you will need to learn to adjust during the game as well.

Here are some common observations where improvement can be made by looking at your past performances:

- Swinging at balls
- Not swinging at strikes
- Swinging and missing in the zone
- Contact on the handle or end of the bat
- Contact of extreme launch angles

Five categories, that's it. You can make this more complicated if you'd like and it might even be recommended if you are moving to the higher levels of baseball to also break these down into different pitch speeds and pitch characteristics, but these five categories are the main things that matter in hitting. By looking at hitting in this way, you can stop with the "I always swing at the ball in the dirt" talk and get more specific with your analysis. Let's dive into each of these.

Swinging at Balls

The pitcher has a job to do and about 17 inches, plus or minus a ball width (the strike zone) to do it with. The pitcher can throw two pitches in the exact same spot and receive one strike and one ball, based on umpire preference. One great thing you can do to help yourself out is to stop swinging at the balls that aren't going to be over that 17-or-so inch wide plate. Also, don't swing at the high and the low ones. Everybody knows this advice but knowing and doing are two different things. Batting practice is the time to get stingy with the pitches you swing at. So, if you are swinging at balls and that is why you aren't getting hits, get to practicing on letting the ugly pitches go and swinging at the pretty ones.

Not Swinging at Strikes

This is the same as above, but the opposite. Is it mandatory that you swing at every strike? No, of course not. This game gives you three opportunities for that, which is another reason the game is so great. However, it is important to swing at enough strikes so an umpire or the pitchers best pitch don't continue to get us out. Put more simply, as the game gets more advanced you can start to look at each at bat like this: one pitch is yours, one pitch is the pitchers, and one pitch is the umpires. So, swing at **your** pitch. Common reasons for not swinging at your pitch include: guessing a pitch is going to come on one corner or the other, guessing a certain speed is going to come and getting a different speed, or attempting to hit a ball to a certain zone on the field and getting a pitch you're unable to hit to that zone. Hit with a clear mind and look for pitches closer to the middle of the zone. That way you can make subtle adjustments in, out, up, or down from the middle rather that key-holing a pitch on the corner of the plate.

Swinging and Missing in the Zone

It's a bad feeling to have that pitch you've been waiting for all day, right down Broadway, only to hear the pop of the catcher's mitt as you finish your swing. The good news is that you're not the first to miss the perfect-looking pitch. The bad news is that if you continue the trend you are going to miss some great opportunities for hits. There are many reasons for missing in zone and they could be the same as the reasons for not swinging at strikes mentioned above or they could also be for other reasons like swinging too hard, swinging too soft, incorrectly gauging the timing of the pitch, or a swing flaw. Although we may be quick to jump to the conclusion of swing flaw, it may be one of the other three culprits. If you have some video to back that you are on time and seem to be keeping an even tempo, it might be time to look at those mechanics and fix something. However, while in the middle of the game if it isn't practical to change your swing, it may be a better adjustment to swing at a different part of the ball to still get some better results. For instance, if you missed under the ball try and swing and miss over the ball or just barely hit the top of the ball. If you're missing in zone, don't assume the worst, you can still find a way to compete.

Contact on the Handle or the End of the Bat

The average baseball bat has about a 3.5-inch margin where the ball is designed to be hit on. We have come to know this as the 'sweet spot' or the barrel. Contact on the end of the bat stinks because it stings a little bit, doesn't go very far, and may break a wooden bat. Contact on the handle can mentally challenge even the most confident of hitters. Many hitters live with a fear of being 'beaten' by the pitch and hitting the ball off the skinny part of the bat. This fear is somewhat rational, but if either of these outcomes are present the hitter should evaluate his targeting on the ball first. Often, the hitter is not accounting for pitch movement or is simply attacking the ball where he is assuming it will be and is taking the bat to the wrong spot. Unfortunately, if this is a common outcome, a swing flaw may be present, and it would be best to start to attack the flaw that is leading to the issue. It is OK to miss sometimes and to even hit the ball on the handle. Continue to adjust to find the barrel and keep running the sweet spot into the baseball as often as possible.

Contact of Extreme Launch Angles

Every batted ball has two different planes it can be hit on when it is hit into the field of play. There is the horizontal plane (left, center, right, etc.) and the vertical plane (fly ball, line drive, ground ball, etc.). The vertical plane is known as the launch angle and can be a good indicator of your swing when you look at the vertical angles the ball is coming off your bat. Line drives are awesome, but if the ball is coming off your bat with pop-ups that are straight up, or ground balls that bounce in the dirt of the hitting area, this may signal an issue. These two outcomes are extreme launch angles and rarely result in hits. If you are consistently hitting balls with extreme launch angles check your focus point on the ball first to see if you can aim at a different part of the ball to get back to hitting line drives. If this doesn't solve your issues you are most likely looking at an issue with your swing and you will want to proceed in a way that gets more consistent contact. There are several different measuring devices for the bat and how it moves through the hitting zone, but my favorite is video because we can look at the movements that lead up to the bat working a certain way. However you feel most comfortable fixing the issue, get to work so you can get back to consistently hard hit balls

These five categories mostly sum up the mistakes hitters make. If you go down the list and look at your performance, you can see the areas of weakness and room for growth in your game. Everybody makes outs sometimes, so don't get overly critical because of a couple of games. And most of all, don't compare yourself to other players. The greatest players in the history of baseball didn't get there by criticizing themselves because they didn't get as many hits as the guy next to them, and you won't either. You will go through stretches where you are hitting great and not getting any hits and you will go through stretches where you are hitting poorly and getting hits. Reflect on your performance and the contact quality so you can get keep improving and shorten stretches of poor performance with the bat.

Section IV: Preparing for Whatever is Next

Chapter Thirteen: Do You Want to Play College Baseball?

High school baseball is an opportunity to develop and demonstrate skills on the field while you also learn to dominate your schoolwork and become a better person. Your goal at the end of high school could be any number of things ranging from entering the workforce, trade school, or college. If you think you might be interested in playing baseball in college, you need to start taking steps to ensure you are on the correct academic path early in your high school years. The number of baseball players who advance as they grow older will shrink with each year and works like a funnel. The drop-off is most significant between high school and college and if you have decided you want to play in college you will be in a select group if you do make it. This chapter is a dive into the ins and outs of college baseball for those who want to continue after high school. When you begin the college recruiting process, use this chapter and the advice to aid your decision.

First Question: Why do you want to go to college?

If you are seeking a specific type of degree, experience, or future outcome you need to make decisions based on this answer. If the school you are seeking doesn't match up with your goals, it should be a 'No' from you right away. If you are seeking a college "experience," it is best to talk with your family about finances and to also make sure you aren't going to put yourself into long term debt because you wanted to go to football games. College can be expensive so don't waste time and money going somewhere that doesn't align with your motivations.

Second: Would you go to the school if you weren't playing baseball?

The reality of the baseball funnel is, after college, very few players move to the professional level and enjoy a career without some other type of work. You will want the degree to apply it to your future in most cases, so make sure you like the school. I will say that most college campuses are awesome in their own ways. College towns have a certain buzz to them with many young people who are working on themselves and their futures. Even the smallest colleges have positive qualities, but you will need to decide if you like the college for yourself.

Third: What is the lifestyle going to look like?

Are you going into a situation with dorm rooms, off campus living, or staying at home? Are you equipped to cook for yourself if you need to? You may need to learn a couple life skills before embarking on your journey to take care of yourself away from your family. Ask the college recruiter if there are weight room hours, what the practice hours are, and if there are any bits of community service you will need to be involved in. At the division I level, it is very difficult, although not impossible, to work any sort of job during the year because of the demanding schedule. At other levels, you may be able to work a job if you need to make extra money, so factor those things in as well. You should have a clear picture of the requirements of the baseball team before you start college, from a time perspective.

Fourth Question: How long has the staff been there, and what are their backgrounds like?

College baseball is an absolute circus for coaching movement. At some schools, the athletic director is looking for a new head coach every 3-4 years because coaches leave for better jobs. At others, you will find an entire staff that has remained at the school for several years. Keep in mind, the recruiter you are talking to may very likely not be coaching you often at practice and may have moved to a different school by the time you arrive on campus. The head coach may be in the same boat as well, so make your decisions accordingly.

Number Five: How many players will be on the roster in your position when you arrive on campus?

Although you will probably not get an answer as to the amount of recruits the school is looking to bring in with you, you can get a feel for who is returning. Recruiters will downplay returning players and will likely tell you the position is always open for competition and one or more returners at your position may not come back but take a look at the stats and see for yourself. Returning players at your position shouldn't scare you, but you will want to be informed before you arrive on campus.

Six: What type of player and person is the college looking for?

Most college coaches have an image of the player they want in their program and you should ask them what that image is. In some cases, schools are looking for a diverse group of personalities, but in others there are some defined characteristics. This question will help you to figure out if you are a fit for that program and that coach. This question is not at the top of the list because you can always grow into the player and person your coach wants, but occasionally you will learn that you don't want to go to the school because of this answer.

Feel free to expand on this question list, but this is something to get you started when you are talking to college recruiters. I want to continue this chapter with some different topics for concern that many different players have, and hopefully give solutions to those concerns.

Concern #1: Money

First and foremost, ask your parents how much they are willing and able to spend on your college per year. Come up with a number that is rock solid. If you won't have any family contribution, make sure you are aware of this before talking about money with a recruiter. Also, find out what type of grant financial aid, not loans, that you will qualify for based on your need. Go to **studentaid.gov** for information and use google as a tool. Remember, loans will need repayment, but grants will not. Money, in my opinion, should be at the forefront of this decision to play baseball in college and you should never wreck your parents' finances or put yourself into a financial hole for the rest of your life to play in college.

Concern #2: Interest

If you are a sophomore in high school and not receiving interest from colleges, that is totally normal! Many college-bound players receive interest at the beginning of their junior year, but you cannot formally sign an NLI (National Letter of Intent) until you are a senior. Many players and parents begin to worry about exposure to colleges at points that are either too early to matter, or too late to help. Before you are a sophomore, do not worry about college interest. If it happens, great, but if not, you have time to impress the right people. If you are late in your high school senior season or the season has ended, you are probably too late to gain interest from division I, II, or even most NAIA schools. Don't worry, there are other options I'll touch on later if you are in this situation. As for ways to build this interest, this is a messy subject, so I figured I'd break it down into sub-categories.

Showcases

Showcases are either tournaments or individual events hosted with the promise of college and possibly pro scouts in attendance. There are many reputable and many non-reputable showcases. In 2021, PBR seems to have showcases dialed in and give the best information regarding your speed, athletic ability, and video to colleges. Perfect Game is another reputable showcase business, but I'm currently seeing them as a close second-place, at the moment. There are many different reputable organizations, but the best way to display your talents is through the tournaments with these organizations. At tournaments, colleges get a chance to see you play in competition as well as some batting practice and running speed tracking before the event starts. Check the event details to find the schedule and talk to the organizer, if possible, so you know what to expect. Don't go to a showcase unless you are physically ready to do so. Trying to show off your best self when you have had several months off is a bad idea.

Recruitment Services

Recruitment services come in many forms, from independent individuals who will help you with your recruitment, to companies dedicated to doing so. My friend, Tony Cappuccilli, assists in recruitment for athletes as an independent at his site **baseballhub.org** and he tells every player this: I don't do anything for you that you couldn't do yourself. He works to guide athletes through contacting schools with professional contact techniques, assists in video and data compilation so it works best for college recruiters, and consults the athletes on the level they may be best currently suited for. Recruitment services cannot guarantee you a scholarship to your dream school but may be a valuable asset to get you an opportunity where you may not have previously had one. It might be a good idea to consult with some of your coaches and others you trust who have played at the level you are aspiring to play before entrusting a recruitment service, because it may save you some money. Some recruitment services can get very pricey and checking the quality of the service beforehand is very difficult. If the recruiting service over-sells you to a college, you could end up with some major issues once you are on campus. Recruitment services may pay off with scholarship dollars, especially if you are flexible on the level and school you are looking to attend.

High School

Your play in high school may help you to attract interest from colleges, especially if the players you are playing against have MLB draft or college recruitment interest as well. If you are playing at a smaller school and the competition is severely below college level, your high school play may have no effect to attract colleges. One thing is certain, your stats in high school don't do much to help. Colleges like to scout high school games because they can see you in competition, but they probably won't see your stats and call you solely based on those.

Travel Ball

Possibly the most hit-and-miss way to get looked at from colleges will be your travel ball team. There are highly reputable travel ball coaches and organizations who can call colleges on your behalf, but these are very rare. Your best bet with travel ball is that your team will play in tournaments against high-level competition and college recruiters will attend. If you can't access a travel team that has the ability to call colleges or to play in high-level tournaments, you may want to go the showcase route for your individual talents.

College Emails

Believe it or not, occasionally colleges do recruit based on the emails they receive. If you are interested in attending a school, there is nothing wrong with emailing the recruiting coordinator and telling them you would like to attend the school and play for them. A couple rules of thumb would be to: 1) Write the email in a professional manner addressed to the recruiter individually and 2) Write your own email, don't let your mom or dad do it. If you can link video to the email, this will help tremendously. Colleges really like to see pitch velocity in the video to gauge the level, so if you have this information it can really help. Exit velocity probably won't help your cause, although giving a college your exit velocity information if it is lower than 75 or 80 mph may hurt your cause. Personally, I'd omit exit velocity altogether and include the velocity of the pitch if it was available, but don't lie or exaggerate the details in these emails.

Social Media

If you have the ability, it is possible to leverage social media to help your cause. Social media recruiting is tricky because you'll need things to look professional and tasteful, while getting your message out to people who can help you. Social media is much easier to use if you are a pitcher, since throwing velocity verified by a radar gun is something a college recruiter is looking for. For a hitter, colleges will want to see that you are able to hit against pitchers with velocity. If you can show video of in-game hitting or live at-bats and there is a way to show the pitcher's velocity as well, but don't guess, this is most useful to a college. Twitter and YouTube are probably your best options in 2021 for social media. If you do want to leverage social media for your recruitment, your profile must be professional and avoid anything that may cause you to lose opportunities.

Concern #3: Playing Time

You should be concerned with your potential for playing time at the college you are planning to attend if you plan on playing on the field during games. With this said, one red flag for players should always be a promise of playing time. You are going into a situation where the best players should play. This is the case because the college coach will typically be reliant on winning to keep his job. It is up to you to develop your skills and earn your way onto the field, but you should also see a realistic path to do so. Many times, playing time as a freshman at the Division I level is hard to come by, but D II, III, NAIA, and JUCO all rely on quality freshman regularly. Be realistic about your chances of playing and make the decision that works best for you.

Concern #4: Opportunities After College

Check up on the players who have played in the program at the school you are looking to attend. Are those people successful in future endeavors? You want to know if the staff is concerned with past players and if the school or program equipped them for success. If you want to play professional baseball, find out how many players have previously done the same from that school and conference within the last five years. Many schools offer unique career opportunities in business or marketing and that may be attractive for you.

Concern #5: Development Opportunity

Each level presents regulations for the number of hours you are able to actually practice with a coach present. Figure out if the school you are attending can allot the time you feel you will need to get the coaching you desire. Also, schools are equipped with different quality facilities depending on the resources of the school. A beautiful weight room is great, but if your team is only inside of it one hour per week because you are required to share with other sports and students it isn't really a factor. Figure out which resources are at your disposal to improve your body, athleticism, mind, and future career potential as these will vary widely between institutions.

Concern #6: Saying 'No'

The best recruiters do an excellent job of building a relationship with the players they are recruiting. In turn, they are able to sign recruits at a high rate because many players make emotional decisions to attend the school. Although this may be the first time in your life to say this word to an authority figure, it is ok to say 'No' to a college recruiter. In fact, recruiters receive many more No's than Yes's. Once you say no to a school because it isn't what you are looking for, they will move to the next recruit on their list of recruits. At the best schools, this is a very long list. The decision to say yes to a school is a life-changing decision and should be considered as such. However, there is a proper way to tell a school you are not interested, and it is to actually tell them you are not interested. Simply avoiding phone calls, texts, or emails is a bad start to your college career, so don't do it. When a school calls, always return the call and tell them the truth about your decisions.

Going to College on Scholarship

Every level is allowed a different number of athletic scholarships. Many schools do offer extra aid based on high school or college-transfer grades, but that is not tied to athletic scholarship and is a separate entity as you will be required to maintain a GPA to keep this extra money. This does not mean the school you are looking at in that level is using that full number of athletic scholarships as this is up to each individual institution, but it does mean the school cannot exceed that number of athletic scholarships. The maximum allowed athletic scholarships at each level are:

4-year Institutions
- NCAA Division I: 11.7
- NCAA Division II: 9
- NCAA Division III: 0
- NAIA: 12

2-Year Institutions
- NJCAA Division I: 24 Full including housing
- NJCAA Division II: 24 Cannot include housing
- NJCAA Division III: 0
- California Community College (CCCAA): 0

*California Residents pay 46 dollars per unit - 60 Units required to graduate. Many local residents to college may have all cost per unit waived in first year. [2]

With these numbers in mind, it is very rare to see a player at a four-year institution on 100 % athletic scholarship in baseball, which is commonplace in many other sports. When you do begin to talk money with a recruiter, ask how many athletic scholarships they are allowed from the school and this can help to understand the situation you are entering and how invested the school is to the baseball program.

This information is based on my previous play at the CCCAA, NCAA Division I, and NAIA levels as well as my experience placing student-athletes in these levels from the junior college level. If you find yourself on the outside looking in with no schools interested in you, a 2-year junior college (JUCO) may be a great route to take an extra 2-3 years to prepare yourself for a four-year school at a cheaper cost. The JUCO option is also great for players looking to improve professional draft status as junior college players may be drafted every year, opposed to NCAA and NAIA regulations which stipulate draft eligibility after junior year or turning 21. A commitment to a 4-year school should be treated with caution, and the same for JUCO.

Now that you are playing baseball in high school you will see other players who are offered an opportunity at a college and will verbally accept that offer. Many players who commit to a school will immediately post an announcement to friends and followers on social media sites. Don't worry if you haven't received any offers and, especially, don't commit to a school to simply post that you've done so. When you commit to a college, you are agreeing to move there, if necessary, and trust the coaching staff to have your best interests in mind. There are players, as young as eighth grade, who have verbally committed to a college before ever playing in high school. These are players with early-developing bodies and skills, and you may be slower to develop. That verbal commitment should be something you stick to, as your word you give others should be extremely important. Remember back to earlier in the book and stop comparing yourself to others. Take care of yourself and keep working to improve. Take time to make decisions for the college you'd like to attend. When the right offer comes your way, you will know.

The Odds

I thought it important to include this section, but mostly for the parents who are reading this. For the players, who cares about the odds of success? The lower the odds, the more you should get excited by the opportunity. However, for parents I want to give realistic details for movement of players beyond the high school levels. Per the NCAA website, 7.3 percent of players who play in high school play at the NCAA level, which doesn't include junior college. Of those 7.3 percent, 9.9 percent move to the professional level. The funnel for high school players started with 482,740 players and lead to 791 players drafted in 2019 which is less than 1 percent of players and around 400 high school players drafted which is much less than 1 percent. The odds are slim but not impossible.[3]

Chapter Fourteen: Managing the Recruiting Process

As you develop your skills and play in more events, you will likely begin to see college coaches in the crowd at your games. These coaches are tasked with finding the next group of players to win baseball games at their respective schools. All recruiters have different styles of recruiting at games and tournaments, from those who will sit right in the middle of the stands with a radar gun and stopwatch, to those who will hide down the line and silently observe. Many recruiters will pop in and out of games and will stay for only a couple innings before heading to the next game. Most college recruiters know what they are looking for when they head out on the road, whether it is a power bat, a defensive shortstop, or an extra player for the college's JV team. You don't need to put on a show when you see a recruiter. Be yourself and play like you always would because they're looking for a player that fits a description and that may or may not be you.

A coach recruiting for a college is going to analyze your tools and the first impression will be like the first impression with your high school coach. If you regularly play in a way you feel wouldn't appear best to a recruiter, start playing like they're always there ASAP. Recruiters do not always get to see you in your most successful games, but they will want certain measurables like your running speed down the line. If you are taking batting practice in front of a college coach it is better to hit the ball hard consistently rather than attempt to hit every ball to the moon and mishit a bunch of pitches. When looking for power bats college coaches typically prefer to see in-game power versus batting practice power. There is never a good time to give up during a play, show poor body language, or cause issues with your coaches or teammates in games...especially when a college coach is in attendance.

If a school decides to contact you or you have decided to reach out to a school, there are ways help your cause. Contact with schools is **much less complicated** than you probably think. If a school sees a player they like, they will find a way to get that player's number and contact them. Often, they will contact your coach first to talk about you, but not always. When a college calls you, there is one golden rule in recruiting: call them back. It doesn't matter if you are already committed to another school, you don't want to go to that college, or have several different offers you are heavily considering. Always call the recruiter back and either explain that you are already committed, are considering offers that are a better fit, or aren't interested in considering attending the school. You might feel like you are giving bad news and delivering a crushing blow to the recruiter, but the truth is a good college recruiter receives many more 'no' answers than 'yes' answers. Calling a recruiter back to talk to them is a basic part of being a good person and, in my experience in baseball so far, the higher the level, the better the people.

Be yourself in the conversation. Trying to impress a college recruiter by over-selling yourself is a very bad idea. Answer questions honestly and if you don't have an answer thought out, respectfully explain you'll need some time to think about your answer and have something ready the next time you speak with that recruiter. You are building some trust with your conversations and although they can feel like a job interview, resist the urge to sell yourself at all costs. You are making a commitment to the school you are talking to for several years in most cases, so speak honestly so both sides make a good decision.

Make sure to talk to the most important coaches at the school you are considering attending. By this, I mean the coach for your position as well as the head coach. It is important to have some rapport built up with these coaches, as the recruiting coordinator may not actually coach you often at practice. If you can speak to the strength coach, if the school has one, do that as well. When you request these conversations, be sure to build a list of 3-4 questions before talking to these coaches. Ideas include daily schedule, expectations, fall/spring schedule, or goals for the team going into the season. Sometimes you may think you are going somewhere to compete for a national championship while the staff has a goal of staying above .500. Your questions should help you but ask things that are important and avoid asking about gear, publicity, or playing time (although asking about opportunity to break a starting lineup through hard work is ok).

Handle text communication in an extremely professional way. Capitalize the first letter in every sentence, place punctuation on the end of sentences without extra spaces, and avoid text speak with single letters or abbreviations. Imagine you are writing in your English class when texting or emailing. Although it is a minor detail, it can go a long way toward showing a college you are willing to put extra effort into your communication. Earlier I said be yourself, and texting or emailing professionally doesn't mean you are acting like somebody different. Trust me. Punctuate and type to the best of your ability and it will only help your chances of finding a good fit for college.

Next, it is ok to reach out to a college via email! Although there is a very good chance this email won't get a response, sending a personalized email to a school you want to attend does occasionally work. These emails should, again, be personalized to the school and express your interest in the school and you should be the one typing them (not Mom or Dad). Also, attach video to the email. Schools want to see the appropriate game speed, so if you have the pitch velocity you are hitting against (on a radar gun, don't estimate) or you are playing in a well-known event, include those details so the school can follow up with the event organizers. Include your defense as well. Schools may or may not want your exit velocity, so if you have it you can include it with video but success against higher velocity pitchers is most desired. If you are a pitcher, schools want to know how hard you throw as well as the shape of your pitches so get video from behind the plate, behind you if possible, and a wider angle shot if you can. Music on the video is ok if you really want to include it, but don't include anything with curse words or hate speech. Stay extremely professional with these emails. For Division I schools, sending them during sophomore/early junior year is a good idea as recruiting classes are typically several years in advance. Division II is probably on the same timeline, although many of these will still recruit seniors for the next year's class. Division III, NAIA, and JUCO will typically look at video regardless of your year. Last thing on email is that if a school responds, stay prompt in your response to them and **stay professional**!

Another thing to consider when speaking with colleges, they will want to know your academic information up front. It is a great idea to stay up to date with your class ranking, GPA, and SAT/ACT scores. If you want to go from high school to a 4-year college, you need to let your high school counselor know your freshman year so you can stay on track to make that happen. Colleges are academic institutions, so your academics come first! If the recruiter spoke with your coach, they likely asked how your academics were first, before talking about anything else.

If you are contacted by a school, keep the information in that conversation between you and the recruiter. If you want to tell your coach and your parents the details, those are great resources, but your teammates and social media don't need to know you've been contacted by a school and/or offered a scholarship. Also, other recruiters may ask for details of your conversations with a certain school. **If they ask**, you can give some details as to the offer you have received from a school but using one scholarship to haggle for more scholarship money from another school is a bad idea. Before talking scholarship dollars, sit down with your family and have a conversation or two to figure out how much aid you will need and the highest level of money, whether out of pocket or via loan, you are willing to pay. It is your choice whether to post offers on social media as has been the trend over the last few years, but there are schools who may see a post and decide not to contact you. Schools are looking for team players and your posts about your scholarship offers scream **ME ME ME**!

Your social media isn't private. Even if you decide to make your social media private, colleges are slick in disguising a fake profile to see your information. If you have social media, observe how college recruiters use the platforms and mirror them. Social media can act as a recruiting aid with platforms like Twitter and tags like @flatgroundbats or @flatgroundapp and it can also show you can present yourself positively to the public if your posts are professional. If you have posts documenting your partying and alcohol/drug use, you can guarantee the schools looking at those posts are crossing you off their recruiting list. If you are receiving a lot of attention for your play, you may have people who attempt to interact with you on social media to try and hurt your career. Be careful with your posts and let the platforms work for you.

In this last section, I wanted to talk about face-to-face contact with recruiters. For those recruiters who have spent time away from families and friends to watch you play, you should always be respectful. If they want to talk with you after a game, always respect their wishes and thank them for taking time out of their schedule to watch you. Listen attentively to them as they talk to you, regardless of how your performance was that day. There are a lot of times when a recruiter will only get one or two chances to see you play in person, and you may not play well. If the recruiter believes in you and knows you will succeed, they will watch for your reaction to failure and your interaction with teammates. To hit this point again, recruiters want to always see energy on the field and aggressive play. If you throw equipment, cuss loudly after striking out, or jog on a ground out you may lose your chance with that school. Make it habit to play hard always so you don't change anything when schools are in attendance.

Although most players have the dream of a signing day and celebration, it is extremely important to know that a college commitment is much more than a single day of celebration. Commitments include scholarship dollars, years of hard work, and an agreement between coaching staff and player. Some schools aren't a proper fit, and that is OK. If you are in a situation with more than one offer, pick the school that fits you best and that you can see yourself thriving for. By understanding the possibility that a school isn't right for you from the beginning, regardless of the name of the university, you take the most important step in building a relationship to a coaching staff and school that will last for a lifetime, if done right. Take it slow, be professional, and be honest in all contacts with colleges.

Chapter Fifteen: The Path of Improvement

As a ballplayer looking to achieve greater success through your practice and determination, it is important that your efforts are made with the goal of improvement in games. Improvements in technique and in your athleticism are great, just make sure they translate directly to the competition. If you are working to improve your practice outcomes and are seeing yourself dominating a practice environment, this does not ensure success in the game. Equating your prowess in practice to future in-game success is what I believe to be the fatal flaw for athletes.

You will, in time, see this play out with those around you. You'll play with the hitter who dominates batting practice, but in the game looks like a fish out of water. The pitcher who throws great in the bullpen but can't throw strikes in the game. Dominating a drill is great, but it doesn't guarantee success in the game unless you are continuing to improve your mental and physical abilities and applying the practice time to the game. One great way to make your practices more game-like is through visualization and using your imagination to simulate fans, umpires, and opponents who are trying to beat you. Put pressure on yourself to complete tasks in practice. Take more time than usual between reps from time to time to simulate plays during the game. Visualization can take your practices to a level where they are getting you ready for games.

You're Not Your Teammates

You may see your teammates and their development and think you're not improving as fast as they are. All players and people are extremely different. Many players who see the best long-term gains will see the worst gains in the short-term. Occasionally, you will get worse before you get better at something. The important thing with your development is that you are consistent with your effort and that you reflect on the success or failure you are seeing.

What You Were, You No Longer Are

Every day you wake up is a day you have an opportunity to improve. The same is true for those whom you compete against. As the saying from Bo Schembechler goes, "Every day you either get better or get worse. You never stay the same."[4] For youth players, not only are your skills changing, but the body is rapidly changing as well. The early bloomers typically have more success than the late bloomers until the bodies catch up to each other down the road. You are on this path of constant change, and for this reason keep your focus on where you are going rather than where you have been. Just because you were hot for two weeks in the 2017 season doesn't mean you were necessarily better at that point than you are now. You may have been making more efficient movements, but they may be movements you aren't capable of now because of injury or fatigue. When you get caught looking back and chasing previous success, you're like a dog chasing its tail. Keep focused on the road ahead.

Don't Believe the Hype

Your friends and family will hopefully have great things to say about you and your game. They may also be some of the most critical people when it comes to your game as well. The truth about your game lies somewhere in the middle and it is only up to you to figure out how you see your abilities and shortfalls. There are great players at each end of the spectrum, from those who groan after each mistake to those who are hyping themselves up every second of the day. There is no right way to look at the game and your play and it is only up to you to decide how you want to go about your business. Whether that means taking negative criticism and adding that to the chip on your shoulder or taking positive messages and adding those to your memory for when you're struggling, the choice is up to you and depends on your personality.

The Game Doesn't Owe You Anything

The game of baseball (also life in general) doesn't owe you anything for the effort you put in. The four outcomes of effort are: work hard and succeed, work hard and fail, slack and succeed, slack and fail. The odds are in your favor if you put in extra effort, but nothing is guaranteed in baseball. Do your best to put yourself in good situations for success and keep doing it over and over. The idea that success will come your way because you are deserving of luck or deserving of sustained success is nonsense. Just stay after it and stay consistent about your work, making small adjustments along the way to gain more success.

Find A Release Mechanism

Baseball absolutely cannot be your only outlet to occupy your time. It can be your favorite one or the one you spend most time with, but you need something else as well. Something as simple as fishing, video games, time with friends, or even exercise can act as positive outlets if they don't detract from your improvement as a baseball player. By having an outlet, you give yourself a worst-case scenario that isn't all that bad like, "If I strike out here at least I will have that hike tomorrow morning." While it is better to have no negative thought in your mind, when they do come up a release mechanism can lower your stress levels and will probably help you in the moment as well as long term. It is healthy to have a passion outside of the game of baseball so you will have something to look forward to when things get tough.

You're the Best, Always

Many great players talk about "belief" that helped them to conquer all the difficult situations on the path to success. For some this is a spiritual belief, but for most this is also a strong belief in themselves. Make a bet on yourself and build that inner belief until it is so strong that nobody can shake you out of it. That fire inside of you is passion, trust, and belief in the work you are doing. Inner passion is built slowly, but like a snowball rolling downhill starts to grow greater and greater in size at a more rapid pace the longer the snowball rolls. One of the themes in this book is that hard work and dedicated focus is the way to improve, but it will take consistency and time to show itself. You're the best, believe it and work for it.

Lastly, Don't Work as a Means to an End

Math is nice because $1 + 1 = 2$. Sports are frustrating because time put in doesn't always mean your desired outcome is achieved. If your thought is to put in a bunch of work so you can put in less work in the future, you've completely missed the point and will likely enjoy a very short and frustrating career in baseball. The effort you put into baseball only grows as you mature and discover new facets of your game. I don't say this to discourage you, quite the opposite. It becomes more fun to work on the nuance of your game when you have more sweat equity invested into it. Think of a beginner skateboarder who is trying to learn to balance on the skateboard and ride it while moving. That is fun if you want to move around, but then imagine a professional skateboarder who has a full bag of tricks and can fly through the air with the skateboard. Just like skateboarding, as you go from novice to expert in baseball you

Chapter Fifteen: The Path of Improvement

discover new things and draw excitement from your continued development. You will never be able to stop working, but if you are working on your game with no end in sight, you won't want to stop.

So, what does the timeline look like for your improvement? I don't know. My assumption is that you'll see incremental improvements as you put more effort into getting better, but sometimes it takes longer than you would like. In my experience, your biggest jumps will come when you least expect it. This may be early on or it may be after quite a bit of time of intentional effort, right at the point of frustration where you feel like quitting. Sometimes you get worse before you get better. Stay after it. Keep grinding, you might be one pitch away from that next level in your game.

Chapter Sixteen: Final Thoughts

I wrote this book with the goal of helping you along in your high school journey to become the player you have dreamt of becoming. High school may take some time to get up to speed with the expectations of the baseball program in addition to the new social dynamics you will be experiencing. If you begin working on yourself and your game with an intentional process, you will see improvement and will probably develop a very mature understanding of yourself and your abilities quicker than your peers. As you begin to understand your process and routine, feel free to share with others if they ask. If others on your team or in your group of friends aren't on board with your goals, move to separate yourself from them. Trust those who have your best interests in mind that fit your athletic and academic goals.

Balancing Social and Athletic Life

There is no perfect answer for balancing sport and non-sport schedules in your day. In general, avoidance of drug and alcohol use by should be a given as these will decrease your athletic ability over time. There is a chance you will meet great athletes who indulge in these activities and may play well despite the bad habits. Find other athletes who choose not to use these substances to spend your time with. Hopefully you will also have friends in your classes who do not play any sports. The same rule applies with these individuals. You are growing up in a distracted world with devices, video game systems, and television programs dedicated to taking your attention. Sticking to a strict schedule with these devices is the best way to go to avoid losing time for training or academics. You will organically begin to act and think like the people you spend the most time around, so pick winners.

Playing Other Sports

I didn't mention playing other sports more than a couple times in this book, but that doesn't mean you should be discouraged from doing so. Playing other sports in the offseason can be extremely beneficial to your athletic development. Baseball, after all, doesn't include all that much running or agility during games or practices. Playing another sport like football or basketball can give you the chance to be a dynamic athlete, which will serve you well on the baseball field. My advice to multisport athletes is to communicate with the baseball coach about these other sports and to throw and hit in addition to training for the sport you are playing. If you are playing a football season in the fall and aren't playing any baseball games until the spring, throwing and hitting aren't necessary until the later parts of the football season. However, if you have identified some major issues in your swing or want to add throwing velocity, you may want to continue throughout the entire football season. Colleges like multisport athletes because they are typically more athletic than the baseball-only player. If you feel like focusing solely on baseball after a couple years of playing other sports, you can always do that and continue the extra agility and speed work.

Sitting the Bench

Sitting on the bench stinks, I know. You may not get the opportunities to play that you want right away. Let the desire to play fuel your workouts. If you see you aren't playing much,

Chapter Sixteen: Final Thoughts

plan high intensity workouts and hitting after games so you are still getting good work in. If you haven't played for several weeks, you may want to ask your coach about it. As stated earlier, your coach is doing the best he or she can and although you may feel like you should be playing, they are trying to win based on the information they have observed. Ask them what you can do to improve yourself with the intention of working on those things. If you are working on your craft consistently, it should be no issue to add another thing to the workload. Communication with your coach is important, but you must give it time before assuming that you are never going to play. Coaches will give players several more chances than you may think the player deserves but leave the coaching and lineup to your coach and do your job to work on yourself. You should never become a problem to your coach or other teammates because of playing time.

Could You Go Pro?

Sure, the odds aren't exactly in your favor, but is it possible to go pro straight out of high school? Absolutely, but the opportunity isn't for everybody. It takes special talent to get drafted, no matter your age. For players that sign professional contracts, life changes drastically. It can be a difficult adjustment to learn to live in hotels, host families, and long bus rides. Some players are better equipped than others to make this lifestyle change and it can be a great thing for those who are ready. You may or may not have an opportunity to play professional baseball directly out of high school, but if it is something you want to do, keep working hard to try to get there.

Enjoy It

Your time in high school is limited to a four-year experience through some of the most formative years you will have in your life. I'll be the first to say there are many different things you won't like in high school, but hopefully you can enjoy more times than you dislike. You will build a bond with your teammates that may continue a lifetime and hopefully push each other to the furthest level possible. You'll want time to move faster than it will seem to be moving at many different times, but all those days in high school are a great opportunity for yourself. Earn great grades, make great friends, and enjoy your time as a high school baseball player.

This concludes the High School Baseball Hitter's Handbook. My hope is that you've been given some tools that will help you through your time in high school and at the next level if that is where you are headed. Stay present in each day and work for the future. Be good to those around you and stay grateful for every opportunity you are given. Thank you for reading, please go to 661hit.com for any additional information or inquiries.

Acknowledgements

I've got many people I'm appreciative of for the direction my life has taken and the opportunities I've been given. My parents, Sheryl and Paul, made everything in my life possible and gave me every opportunity to succeed and I am forever grateful.

My wife, Jacqueline, who has supported me in all of my coaching ventures and decisions deserves a special thank you.

Special shout out to Brandon Boren and Tony Cappuccilli for their help with this book. I've learned a ton from both of you that I've used for this book and in my life on a consistent basis.

Thank you to all of my past coaches, especially Tim Painton, John Russo, and Bryan Lewallyn. And of course, my high school coach, Dan Lemon as well. I wasn't always an easy player and bless you all for spending your lives to help those like me.

Thank you to all of the people at Bakersfield College and those at the Delano satellite campus for making work a great place during my time with you.

Thank you to every player I've been lucky enough to coach. I've needed you guys a lot more than you needed me and I pray I've helped you along to keep growing as a person.

Lastly, thank you to everybody in the Dodgers organization and especially Brant Brown and Will Rhymes for taking a chance on me. The Dodgers are an absolute world class organization, and I am so blessed to call my job "work."

References

1. Miller, Randy (2020). *17 Yankees reactions to Derek Jeter being elected to Hall of Fame.* Accessed February 3 2021 through https://www.nj.com/yankees/2020/01/17-yankees-reactions-to-derek-jeter-being-elected-to-hall-of-fame.html

2. Accessed February 3 2021 through https://keepplayingbaseball.org/college-baseball-scholarship-limits-and-rules-by-level/

3. Accessed February 3 2021 through https://www.ncaa.org/about/resources/research/baseball-probability-competing-beyond-high-school

4. Schembechler, Bo and Bacon, John (2007). *Bo's Lasting Lessons.* (1st Edition). New York: Business Plus.

Made in the USA
Monee, IL
03 August 2022